Visual Communication
From theory to practice

Front matter
Communication
Culture
Conflict
End matter

Jonathan Baldwin/Lucienne Roberts

24.99

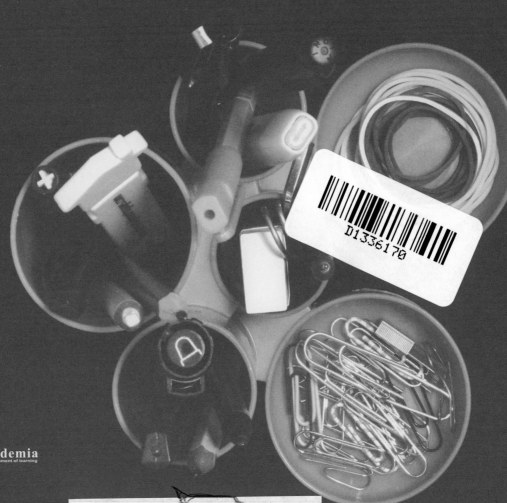

D1336170

ava | **Academia**
the environment of learning

An AVA book

published by
AVA Publishing SA
Rue des Fontenailles 16
Case Postale
1000 Lausanne 6
t: +41 786 005 109
e: enquiries@avabooks.ch

distributed by
ex-North America
Thames & Hudson
181a High Holborn
London WC1V 7QX
t: +44 20 7845 5000
f: +44 20 7845 5055
e: sales@thameshudson.co.uk
www.thamesandhudson.com

English language
Support Office
AVA Publishing (UK) Ltd.
t: +44 1903 204 455
e: enquiries@avabooks.co.uk

design/art direction
Bob Wilkinson
sans+baum

index
Courtesy of Indexing Specialists

production/separations
AVA Book Production Pte. Ltd.
Singapore
t: +65 6334 8173
f: +65 6334 0752
e: production@avabooks.com.sg

ISBN 2-940373-09-4

10 9 8 7 6 5 4 3 2 1

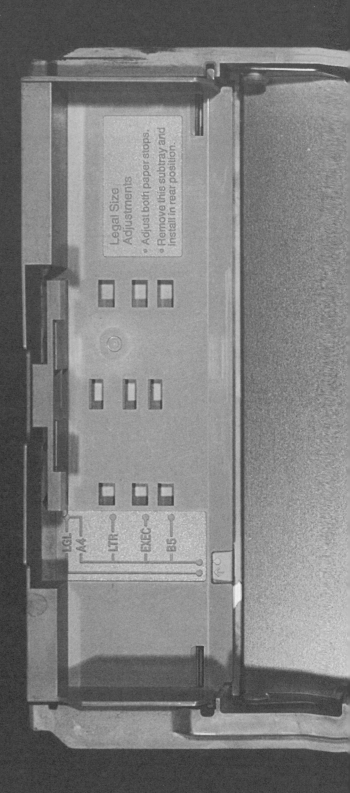

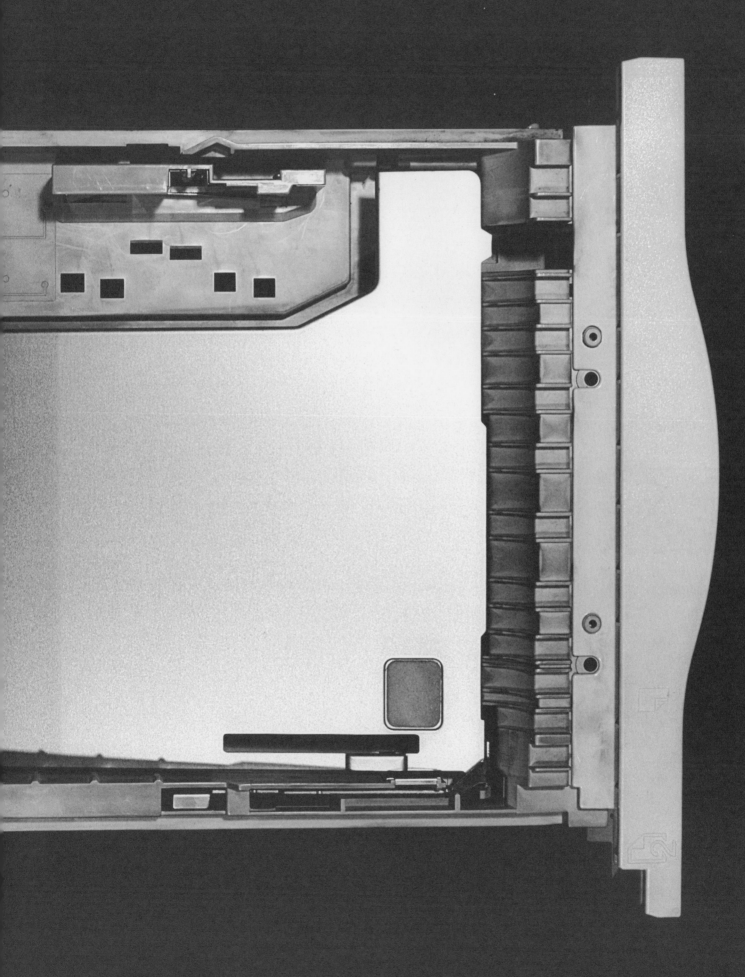

00088354900l0

Acknowledgements
Jonathan Baldwin

I would like to thank the following
people for their help (willing or
otherwise) in producing this book.

Students past and present at
Reading College, Surrey Institute
and the University of Brighton
for allowing me to bore you
with my arguments, and for
a few of your own – in particular:
Carrie May, Lynn Kirkwood,
James Hurst, Charlotte Tassell,
Jasmine Raznahan, Rebecca
Callinan, Shaun Morrison,
Lizzie Osbaldestone and all the
rest for whom the phrase 'I'm
writing a book at the moment...'
must be overfamiliar.'

Special thanks to Natalia Price-
Cabrera, Brian Morris, Renee
Last, Kate Shanahan and Kylie
Johnston at AVA Publishing, and
co-author Lucienne Roberts.

I would also like to thank my
University of Brighton colleagues
(especially Paul Clark, Bruce
Brown, Sarah McLean and Linda
Drew) and my friends Anna
Glanville-Smith, Paula Wilcock
and Cathryn Fogg.

Acknowledgements
Lucienne Roberts

My thanks must go to the
practitioner contributors who
gave their time so willingly
and without whom my sections
of this book would not have
been possible: Neville Brody,
Michael Bierut, Joan Farrer,
Shin Azumi, Tomoko Azumi,
Erik Spiekermann and
Emmi Salonen.

I would also like to thank
AVA Publishing for running
with this approach in the
first place, Teal Triggs for her
help and advice, co-author
Jonathan Baldwin, Rebecca
Wright for being a great friend
and colleague, and everyone
at AVA Publishing, most
particularly Brian Morris,
Natalia Price-Cabrera and
Kate Shanahan.

Lastly, huge thanks go to
Bob Wilkinson: all the late
nights were worth it.

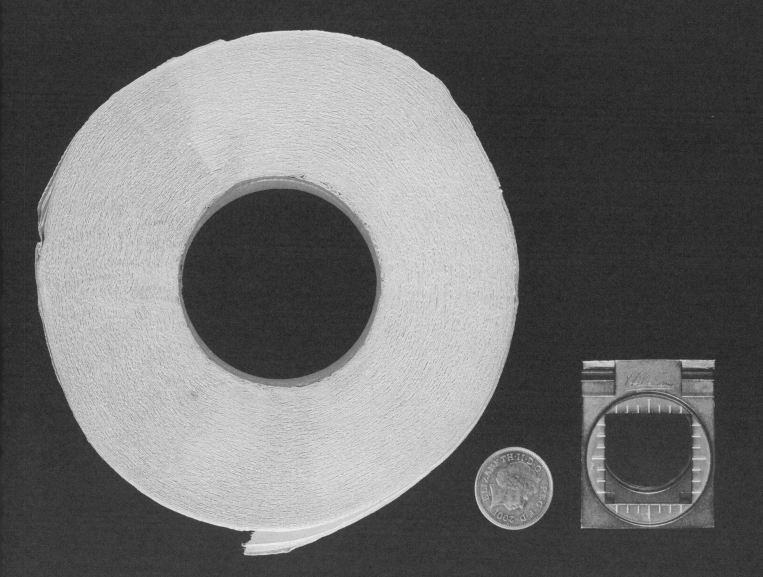

Contents

Front matter

Communication

Culture

Conflict

End matter

How to use this book

Each of the three chapters in this book is split into two halves. The first half is a theoretical essay, carefully written and illustrated to best explain the abstract ideas that underpin the commercial arts, and, in particular, graphic design. The second half of each chapter gives designers experienced in design, whose work is most relevant to the theories discussed, a chance to respond to the theories. In this way, students can judge for themselves how the theories, often borrowed from other related disciplines, can be of use in their own work.

Chapter opener
Each of the three chapters has an opener page like this. On it are listed the educational aims of The Theory text and a summary of the main areas discussed in The Practice interviews. The navigational block at the top indicates clearly where you are within the whole book.

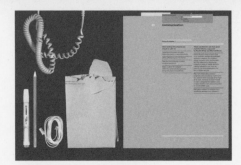

The Theory introduction
The chapter starts with a brief introduction to The Theory essay. This focuses on the most salient points of the text that follows. From hereon the navigational block at the top indicates clearly where you are within the theoretical text of this chapter.

The Theory essay
Each theoretical essay is highly illustrated using a variety of figures, tables and photographs. All levels of heading fall at the top of the page to aid navigation. There are marginal notes throughout the text. For easy cross-referencing these always fall near the relevant text.

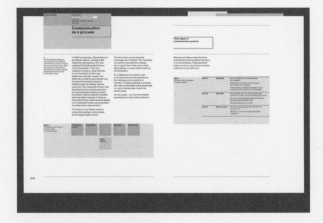

Images run along the top and bottom of the pages, often contained within coloured image zones with the related captions.

The Theory afterword
The theoretical text finishes with a brief summary of what has been covered and the main questions it has raised.

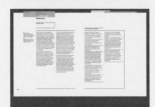

The Practice introduction
The second half of each chapter is comprised of two interviews with design practitioners or design teams. The first spread of this section introduces readers to the theoretical ideas discussed in the interviews and gives some background to the interviewees. From hereon the navigational block at the top indicates clearly where you are within The Practice section of the chapter.

The Practice biography
Preceding each interview are the practitioner's biographical details and a page of images to give a flavour of their work.

The Practice interview
The interviews are highly illustrated. Projects are shown either in an image zone at the top of the page or for more in-depth analysis have a spread to themselves.

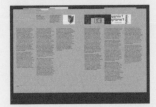

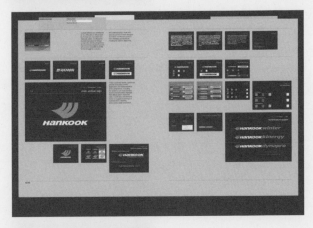

Chapter close
The last page of each chapter raises questions. Some are provocative. They are designed to be a catalyst to further enquiry and debate, making clear the relevance of each chapter to all designers and their practice.

Foreword:
Isn't design simply all about 'the visual'?

Jonathan Baldwin

Theory is an unfortunate term. It suggests something that is unreal or unproven, and of little consequence except to those who like to read long-winded books, engage in intellectual discussions and write long academic essays. At the end of the day, design[1] is all about the visual, isn't it?

Far from it. It's like saying 'making cars is all about speed'. I've chosen the car analogy deliberately because one of the things I've noticed amongst design students recently is a renewed scepticism about the world in which we live, and an engagement with environmentalism, sustainability and anti-globalisation. Indeed, these issues, and the role of designers in them, are discussed in chapter 3. For now, though, I want you to consider an imaginary course in transport-based engineering (cars, trains, planes and so on). As well as all the expected curriculum aspects to do with how machines work, I think it would be a fairly safe bet that you would hope the course covers such issues as:

The **political** implications of transport – government policies, world trade in parts and labour, fuel consumption, public subsidies, private versus public transport, taxation, etc.

The **environmental** issues related to transport – renewable energies, sustainability, recycling, fossil fuels, the impact of drilling for oil and mining for coal, etc.

The **social** impact of transport – the positives such as improved communication, the reduction of isolation, improved mobility for the poor, elderly, disabled; the negatives such as cultural homogeneity, loss of identity, rise in property prices as commuters take over villages and push out families who have lived there for generations.

The effects of **technology** – again, the positives such as reductions in cost, improvements in environmental impact; and the negatives such as increases in use of modes of transport to access areas of the world so far relatively unscathed by mankind.

These four areas – politics, environment, society and technology[2] – can be reduced to the acronym PEST (or STEP if you prefer). It is not a difficult case to make that these issues should be central to the education of budding engineers, civil servants, politicians, architects, and to countless other professions, including design.

Fashion, graphics, products, packaging – all types of design have an impact on the world no matter how insignificant you think they are. As this book shows, design is a form of communication and communication is the basis of our relationships and our understanding of the world. It affects and is used by the world of politics; it contributes to environmental issues[3], but also promises to educate people on them as well; it forms part of the social glue that keeps us together or drives us apart; and as well as being greatly affected by technology it also helps people access it (or prevents them when it is done badly).

Without a consideration of these four areas then, yes, design is purely visual – and arguably completely irrelevant and self-serving. Far from asking 'what's the point of theory?', we should be asking 'what's the point of design without an understanding of how it works?'

One counter-argument commonly heard is that these things are 'obvious', or 'common sense'. Well, it was obvious that apples fall to the ground, but until Newton worked out why it didn't get us very far. At the time of writing we've just landed on another planet's moon, crashed a probe into a comet, and sent a spacecraft bearing messages of goodwill spinning out of the solar system – all because 'the obvious' and 'common sense' was explained. But, more seriously, as you will see, the book returns in each chapter to the statement that 'all design is political', by which I mean the broader sense of the word 'political'. Because visual communication is everywhere we tend to take it for granted in much the same way as we breathe the air around us. We grow up with it, we accept it as natural. And just as the air potentially contains harmful but invisible elements, so our visual atmosphere potentially contains things that are not good for us. Unanalysed they become even more dangerous. It is vital that we understand our visual environment because just as our physical environment keeps us alive, it is our visual environment that makes by far the largest contribution to our relationships with and understanding of the world. Just as we would expect an engineer to be aware of the contribution (harmful or otherwise) they are making to our atmosphere, so designers should be aware of their own contribution to the visual world[4].

If you are studying design, or are a practitioner, this book aims to outline the powerful effects that design can have and show you why. Unlike countless other books on the market it doesn't promise to show you how to produce 'good' design, but it does offer ideas about what makes good design – and it isn't all to do with aesthetics. Some of the topics are deliberately controversial and all are deliberately only dealt with at an introductory level because the book has four main aims:

To provoke you into thinking and talking about design rather than just 'doing' it.

To encourage you to pursue the issues in more depth.

To form your own conclusions independently of academics and practitioners, even if you end up disagreeing with the arguments made here.

To experiment with some of the ideas to see how (or if) they work in practice.

Owning this book is only the first step – the next is up to you. Visual communication offers so much potential to educate, inform, improve and benefit; but these things don't happen by accident. Knowledge, as they say, is power.

1
This book uses the terms 'visual communication' and 'design' interchangeably throughout – but this does not exclude illustration, television or film; the issues covered in this book apply equally, if not more so, to these areas.

2
If you have taken business studies courses you may have encountered these before, but with 'economy' in the place of 'environment'. Here, I've rolled economic considerations into politics and society, and emphasised the environment.

3
For example, graphic designers who work with print directly contribute to the massive amount of waste we produce and, through their choice of inks, create millions of litres of polluted waste water. Making simple choices about the type of paper stock and ink they use could make a significant contribution to the environment. All design students should know these things.

4
Designers have been called 'memetic engineers' because they produce 'memes' or units of cultural information that are recreated and evolve. See *The Selfish Gene* by Richard Dawkins (Oxford: Oxford University Press, 1989) for more on memes.

The Practice

Foreword

The intention of this book is to explore how practice and theory connect and to demonstrate the value of a dialogue between the two. Many academics argue that this symbiosis is already recognised and respected, and yet designers often seem wary of theoreticians. 'They don't use the same language. Our students understand the visual, but not the ideology,' Joan Farrer, practitioner-contributor to chapter 2, explains. She is allowed to be this bold. She has a foot in both camps, researcher at London's Royal College of Art one minute and fashion, textile and branding consultant to retailers such as Marks & Spencer and Virgin Stores the next.

These misunderstandings are easy to explain. Art schools had long been the refuge of idiosyncratic types who didn't fit at university, with tutors who did not see themselves as professional educators, but rather as artists and designers. However, over the last 40 years design education has moved away from non-academic, craft-based practical teaching. The introduction of standardised qualifications and ratification processes has made academic attainment a prerequisite of passing any design course. There is some way to go before this settles down, and the legacy is that design theory and practice can be slightly uneasy bedfellows.

This situation is compounded by the relative youth of what is now deemed to be design practice. The focus of this book is graphic design, which is still in its infancy. Graphic designers themselves are unsure as to their remit and it is an undeveloped area of academic study. 'Ours is a very small and young business,' explains Erik Spiekermann, graphic designer and practitioner-contributor to chapter 3. 'If you talk about classical music, literature or art there's such a body of knowledge and writings that explore different theoretical approaches, but in our business there's nothing really.'

The three chapters of this book are each subdivided into theory and practice. For each chapter, two practitioners or teams of practitioners are invited to comment on the areas explored in the corresponding theoretical text and consider how much one informs the other. Theory should provoke thought about design, but cannot be prescriptive since there are countless ways of adequately solving a design problem. It isn't possible to say that by applying this theory you will always get this result and that it will be 'right'. This is demonstrated by the alternative readings of each practitioner.

Chapter 1, for example, looks at communication theory. Two graphic designers consider this text: Neville Brody from the UK and American Michael Bierut. Their comments make a particularly well-balanced read. Brody explains how he rejected some of the more dogmatic approach of his tutors. He was taught that a designer should take a position of neutrality in the communication process, but he questioned this, arguing that objectivity is impossible to achieve and that it is a con to pretend otherwise. Bierut comments that 'putting a high premium on self-expression in design has become dogma on its own. The third path is to get beyond external rules and internal impulses and focus on two things that are often neglected by both camps: the content of the work and the audience we are supposed to be communicating with.'

There is one notion that is common to all three chapters: that design is a political activity. Bierut sums up why with great clarity. 'Much, if not most, graphic design is about communicating messages, and many of those messages are intended to persuade,' he says. 'This places its practice clearly in the realm of politics, broadly defined, even when the message is not about "political" issues.'

Chapter 2 looks at design for the mass and exclusive markets, sub- and counter-cultures and how the public assert themselves by appropriating designers' work. A designer's target audience reveals their world view, but designers must also recognise that their work has a meaning that is determined by the recipient. The practitioners who considered this text come from the worlds of fashion and furniture and product design. Joan Farrer from the UK talks about her experience in fashion and textiles, working for the major high-street retailers, alongside raising awareness of waste and issues of sustainability. She discusses the long lead times, cut-throat pricing and the global aspects of the fashion industry – the behind-the-scenes workings that are a revelation. Japanese product and furniture designers Shin Azumi and Tomoko Azumi also comment in chapter 2. They have worked for Muji and Habitat on the high street as well as more high-end manufacturers, but approach all their work with a highly democratic philosophy.

Chapter 3 looks more closely at this subject. The practitioners who consider the theory in relation to their practice are Erik Spiekermann from Germany and Emmi Salonen from Finland. Salonen is an idealist. She protests actively and has tried various ways to ally her political agenda with her work. Her experiences have taught her that political engagement can be played out with a small 'p'. 'I realise that I don't have to do work about anti-globalisation or war to be social and political,' she says. Spiekermann meanwhile is pragmatic. He signed the First Things First manifesto in 2000, a call for designers to take more social responsibility in their work. Spiekermann considers this to be an ideal that can never be put universally into practice, but signed it wishing that it could be so.

Practitioners are right to worry that academic study of what is essentially a hands-on subject is removing it from the reality of practice. However, this theoretical text juxtaposes the academic with the 'real' world, making it accessible, easy to assimilate and relevant. Jonathan Baldwin points out in his introduction that an understanding of theory helps designers recognise the potential of their work and that this is empowering. A designer is not just the person who applies the metaphorical icing on the cake, but clients will only understand this potentially expansive role if designers are aware of it first. Designers tend to work instinctively, without appearing to knowingly apply theory, but often recognising it after the fact.

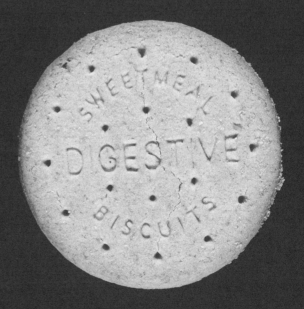

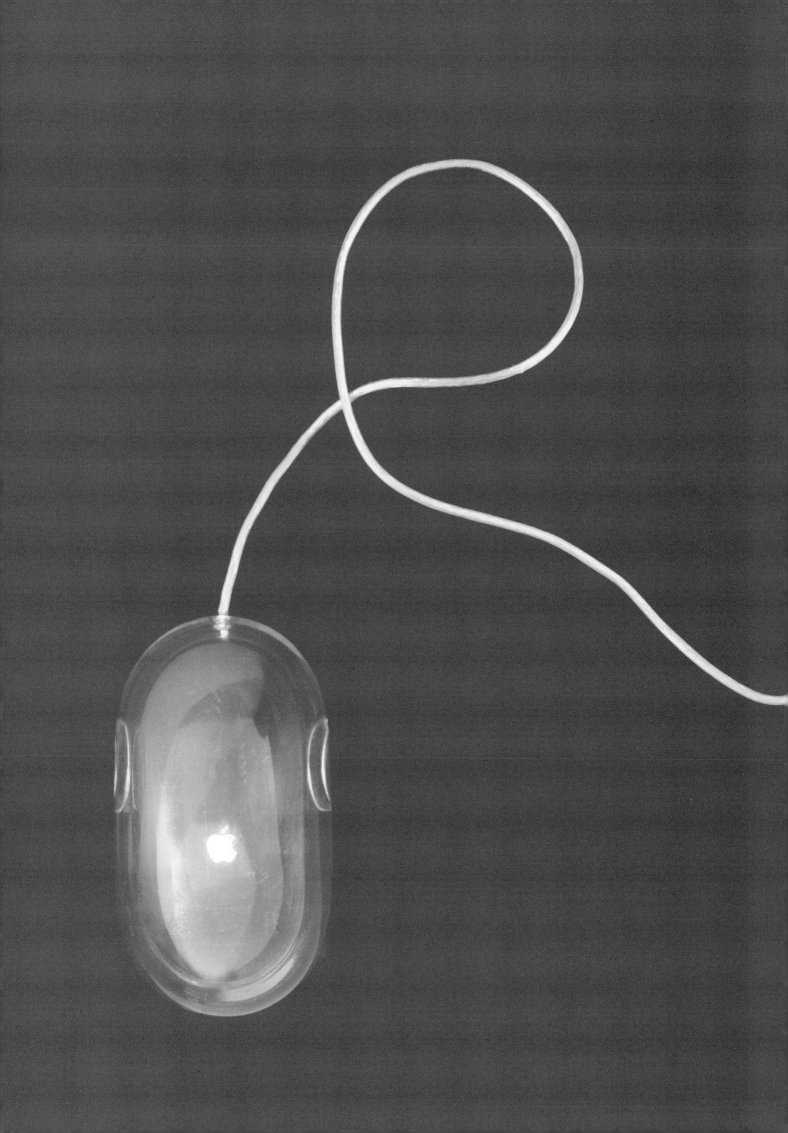

please return to:
840, Warrington, WA1 1WT

Visual Communication
Front matter
01 Communication
02 Culture
03 Conflict
End matter

01 **Communication**

Aims of chapter 1

After reading this chapter you should be able to:

Understand the basic concepts of process theory in communications.

Define different types of audience.

Describe how language is based on signs (semiotics).

Begin to place the designer within the communication process, along with client and audience.

These key theories are then given real-life industry responses by Neville Brody and Michael Bierut:

Neville Brody is wary of theory that is too dogmatic, seeing it as potentially limiting to creativity. He considers design neutrality to be unachievable and that attempts to disguise the subjective nature of design decision-making mislead the end-user. He believes that appropriateness is the key to design success.

New York-based Bierut takes a pragmatic view and places content and the recipient of the message at the heart of his work. However, he doesn't want to overly categorise the audience and is happy that his work will be interpreted in uncontrollable ways.

Education comes in for criticism too – something we return to in chapter 3.

The Theory

Introduction

**Even natural processes
have explanations**

In this first chapter I want to outline two approaches to communication theory that stem not from a study of the visual, but from the worlds of technology and linguistics. That's because the visual arts and crafts borrow heavily from areas such as psychology, sociology, politics, and media and communications studies for many of the theories that help to explain how they work. There is, however, often a strong resistance to attempts to explain the apparently inexplicable. Reasons for this will be explored in more depth in the third chapter, but as Lucienne Roberts points out in her introduction to the first two interviews, the real world of design work is often harsher and more practical than it is made out to be by those who teach it, write about it, or who can afford to pick and choose the design jobs they do. The field of visual communication is unromantic – it isn't concerned with star names and big agencies or fashion houses, but with everyday design, everyday people, and everyday communications.

The fact is, visual communication operates in some way – quite what that way is forms the focus of communication theory (or to be more precise, theories); those discussed here are just a sample and there are many more, some of them competing, contradicting or reinforcing each other. In this chapter we look at visual communication from two angles. The first, derived from information technology, views communication as a linear process in which a message or idea is passed from A to B. The second approach, courtesy of linguistics, views communication as the production of meaning and suggests that one message is going to mean different things to different people depending on lots of different factors.

The first approach is called 'process theory' and places the emphasis on the sender and the channel or medium used for the message; the second is known as 'semiotics' and focuses on the receiver and the social, political and economic environment in which they live. Although both are often seen as competing models of communication they actually have a great deal in common and are worth considering as complementary rather than opposing theories. Both have important implications for the producers of visual communication because they suggest a political role for design, something we shall return to throughout the book.

Often graphic and advertising design are seen as the most natural fits to the theories discussed in this chapter, with the result that fashion designers, product designers, illustrators and so on might imagine they have no relevance to them. In fact the theories do – as we will see in the last section of this chapter, and throughout the book.

Keywords in this chapter

Process theory
The idea that communication can be described as a linear process, with a direct path from the sender of a message to the receiver.

Semantics
The meaning of a word or symbol.

Client
In the context of this book, the person or organisation who initiates a design or communication.

Audience
The group or individual who receives a message, usually intentionally targeted.

Text
Any cultural artefact, such as a book, record or film.

Reader
The person who consumes the text and creates or uncovers the meaning it contains.

Feedback
In communication, the method by which we know our message is being received and the effect it is having.

Noise
Anything that gets in the way of, or distorts, a signal and potentially alters the understanding of our message.

Class
Traditionally the social order and hierarchy, but in this book 'class' is a means of distinguishing between broad groups of people based on income, lifestyle and values without making judgements.

Redundancy
A feature of a message that could be left out, but which helps the message to be understood. Clichés are an example of redundancy.

Entropy
Technically, entropy is the rate of transfer of information. A highly entropic message is transferred quickly, but because it lacks redundant elements it is more likely to be misunderstood.

Semiotics
The study of signs and symbols, their meanings and uses.

Marxism
A theory of social change that focuses on economics and in which the production and consumption of goods and cultural texts contributes to the political and ideological structure of society.

Communication

Introduction
Communication as a process
Semiotics
All design is political: part one
Afterword

Communication as a process

5
The Mathematical Theory of Communication by W Weaver and CE Shannon (Urbana, Illinois: University of Illinois Press, 1949) – this can be downloaded from the internet, but it's an extremely technical document and not for the faint of heart.

In 1949 two engineers, Claude Shannon and Warren Weaver, working at Bell Telephone Laboratories in the USA, published *The Mathematical Theory of Communication*[5]. Their work originally focused on using methods of communication (in their case telephones and radio waves) most effectively, so that the growing demand for telecommunications could be satisfied using the existing network resources. They developed a theory that illustrated how to compress and send as much information down a channel as possible without losing the essential parts that affect meaning. In doing so, they claimed their model could be applied to all methods of human communication – including visual communication.

The Shannon and Weaver model is wonderfully (perhaps overly) simple; as the diagram below shows.

The information source transmits a message via a 'channel'. The transmitter converts (or encodes) the message into a 'signal' that is then reconverted (decoded) by a receiver before reaching the destination.

So a telephone conversation uses a microphone to encode and transmit the message and an earpiece to decode it. A radio broadcast is encoded into radio waves before being transmitted to a tuner that decodes it back into sound waves.

All very simple – but even the simplest processes have their built-in problems.

Figure 1
The Shannon and Weaver process model of communication.

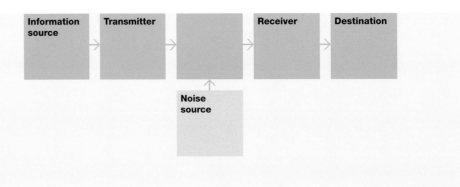

Three types of communication problem

Shannon and Weaver describe three interrelated levels of problem that occur in communications. These questions apply as much to visual communication as they do to any other sort.

Table 1
The three levels of problem in communication.

Level A	**Technical**	How accurately can we communicate our message?
		What system should we use to 'encode' and 'decode' our message?
		Is that system universally compatible or does it require special equipment or knowledge?
Level B	**Semantic**	How precisely does our choice of language, symbols or codes convey the meaning we intend?
		How much of the message can be lost without the meaning being lost as well?
		What language should we use?
Level C	**Effectiveness**	Does the message affect behaviour the way we want it to?
		What can we do if the required effect fails to happen?

Communication

Introduction
Communication as a process
Semiotics
All design is political: part one
Afterword

Client, designer and audience

6
For an excellent discussion
of the design process, see
Visual Research by Ian Noble
and Russell Bestley (Lausanne,
Switzerland: AVA Publishing
SA, 2005) pp 30–41.

7
Sometimes of course the client
and the designer is the same
person. See chapter 3 for a
discussion of design authorship.

8
Marshall McLuhan (1911–1980),
Canadian academic and writer,
is regarded as a founder of
media studies. As well as coining
the term 'the medium is the
message' he also came up
with the phrase 'the global village'
to describe the way in which
mass communications were
changing the world.

Attempts to model the design process
are never satisfactory (and many
designers reject the notion that they
work to a process at all), but the
simplicity of Shannon and Weaver's
model is attractive[6].

In the model below the client's message
or idea is encoded by the designer[7].
We can see that the way the message
is disseminated also has an effect on
the decoding process – one TV channel
or chain of shops may be seen as
more authoritative or of a higher quality
than another, while a broadsheet
newspaper and a tabloid will have
different effects on the message received,
even though the message and the design
remain identical. Marshall McLuhan[8]
most famously encapsulated this in the
phrase 'the medium is the message'.

The designer's domain is largely the
semantic level of communication, given
the role of conveying the intended
meaning, being careful not to change
it or add to it, while possibly strengthening
it. But as the three levels operate together,
it's important the designer understands
the decisions that affect the other two
levels as they ultimately affect the design.

Figure 2
The commercial visual
communication process.

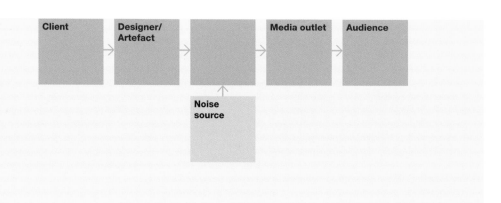

Tackling the technical level

Technical decisions are often, though not always, made before designers become involved. Some designers have what is often known as 'upstream involvement', meaning they are included in or even responsible for decisions regarding the technical level. Others are kept out of (or happily stay out of) such matters.

So what is the technical level in design? In graphic design and advertising a decision will be made early on about the best way of communicating with a particular group of people. Depending on whom the target audience is, technical choices will include whether to use TV, radio, posters, PR, national or local press, consumer or professional magazines, the web, or below-the-line[9] promotions such as competitions, price offers and so on. For example, there's no point using bus shelter ads to promote a prestige fashion product, as in theory the users of public transport tend not to be the sort of people who buy such things. In the same way a value supermarket chain might find bus shelters more effective than an expensive website (generalisations like this are dealt with later). Sometimes designers are involved in these decisions, but not always – somebody else in the process such as a buyer, printer or colourist may determine the cloth or colours used in a fashion collection, or the weight of paper a brochure is printed on. It can be frustrating for a designer to be excluded from these decisions, but more often than not, the relationship is a collaborative one with input from everyone involved.

9
Until recently, advertising agencies would be paid commission by media owners for space or air-time they booked on behalf of their clients. This commission would be credited back to the client in the form of a deduction. Any work like this would traditionally be listed in the top half of an invoice, above the fold (therefore 'above the line') and other work would be listed 'below the line'. The terms are still widely used to group different types of promotional activity.

Communication

Introduction
Communication as a process
Semiotics
All design is political: part one
Afterword

Tackling the effectiveness level

Effectiveness is an important consideration in any form of communication and usually relies on 'feedback', something that Shannon and Weaver ignored in their original research. In verbal communications we receive feedback through body language, eye contact and so on. If you have ever had a telephone conversation with somebody who remains silent throughout, or a face-to-face conversation with someone who keeps a fixed expression throughout, you will know how difficult a lack of feedback can make things. Feedback allows the person sending the message to determine how effective they are being, and to modify things if necessary.

In visual communication professional researchers often gauge effectiveness, but their role is more wide-ranging. In the early stages of a project they work on the technical issues as well as predicting which channels will be most effective with certain audiences. During the design phase they test initial concepts by using a mixture of experience and focus groups. The results of this can help shape the design and determine which concepts go forward[10]. Focus groups need to be set up carefully otherwise they tend to produce 'safe' answers, and many designers have had bad experiences. Resentment can breed among some designers when someone who is not a designer tells them their ideas don't work, and it isn't unusual for the audience to be blamed if this is the case – they just don't 'get' it, it might be claimed. This attitude is partly explained in chapter 3.

After a design has been released, feedback is still gathered to check if the message is being communicated effectively (sales figures being the simplest indicator). If not, the design may be 'pulled' or modified, or simply reinforced through expanded coverage.

10
See chapter 4 of *Visual Research* by Ian Noble and Russell Bestley (Lausanne, Switzerland: AVA Publishing SA, 2005) for more on testing design for effectiveness.

Verbal communications are normally accompanied with visual feedback, made using the body language of gestures. These are culturally based, so that a gesture may mean different things in different cultures. Shaking one's head from side to side in Europe means 'no', but in India, it means 'yes'.

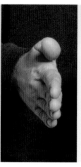

Some designers dislike the idea of getting feedback, but like it or not it will happen in one form or another and rejecting it is the equivalent of talking to yourself. Better to check before you roll out an idea than find out afterwards that it doesn't work. In 1998–99 the UK supermarket chain Sainsbury's ran an expensive advertising campaign called 'value to shout about' using the popular actor John Cleese. In the ads he played a bossy store manager shouting at his staff – but the ads actually resulted in a drop in sales because they made Sainsbury's look incompetent and unsympathetic. The failure to test the ads properly (after all, on paper they sounded like sure-fire winners) allegedly led to Sainsbury's firing the advertising agency responsible.

We can now modify Shannon and Weaver's communication model to better reflect the discussion so far (Figure 3).

As you can see, the designer is just one part of a larger team concerned with getting the mix of technical, semantic and effectiveness levels right. Key to this is the final link in the communication process – the recipient of the message or 'audience'. Identifying the intended audience, and what types of message and media they respond to best, is an important part of visual communication.

Figure 3
Technical, effectiveness and semantic levels added to the model – the designer's role seems to be increasingly diminished.

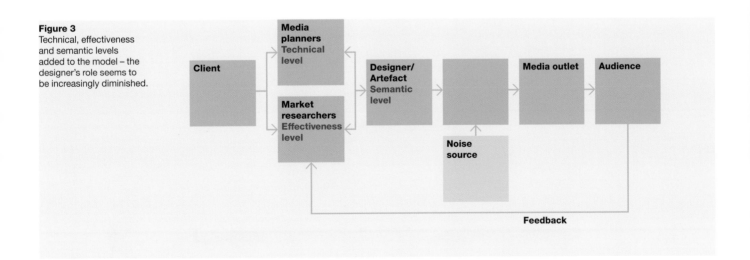

Communication

Introduction
Communication as a process
Semiotics
All design is political: part one
Afterword

Describing audiences

Why focus on an audience?

11
p=m/a formula
(pressure = mass/area).

In an age when mass communication is ridiculously easy it may come as a surprise to hear that not communicating to the masses, but narrowing your audience as much as possible, is a way of ensuring a message gets through relatively unscathed. A design aimed at a specific audience will have more effect than when aimed at a wide one. Knowing your audience is key to successful design. Guessing, or ignoring, the tastes of your audience is potentially disastrous.

Applying the pressure

Imagine being in a room with wooden floors when a 50kg woman wearing stiletto heels leads in a two-tonne elephant. Visually, the elephant will have the greater impact, but the next day the only sign that anything odd happened would be the dents made by the woman's heels. Although the woman weighs less than the elephant all her mass is focused on two small points, while the elephant's is spread out. This physical principle, that pressure is inversely proportional to the area to which a mass is applied[11], is used to great effect by pressure groups (hence the name). Targeting a single issue, or group of people, will have more effect than spreading yourself thinly, and it's cheaper too.

Newspapers offer an easy example of the way in which design signals to its intended audience. *The Wall Street Journal* offers busy readers a quick digest for information grazers who don't have time to wade through everything. The *Daily Telegraph* suggests a more serious tone than the tabloids (but note the colourful banner about inheritance tax – something of concern to the older and/or wealthier demographic to which this paper appeals). The tabloids on the other hand focus on celebrities and short, sensational headlines.

For every interest there is a magazine. Most newsagents can't afford to stock the thousands of titles available but because of the precise nature of this magazine's audience it will depend on, and benefit from, a detailed subscriber database.

Magazines are largely funded by advertisers, not the cover price, and many advertisers would prefer to be able to speak to a tightly defined audience than spend money in bigger circulation publications where the message will be diluted.

How audiences are described

Early newspaper and magazine readership surveys in the UK used categories such as 'housewives', 'heads of household', 'smokers' and 'people with gardens' as descriptions for readers. These crude categories were useful to advertisers who wanted to target those people and could use them to decide where to spend their money. Today the UK's National Readership Survey (NRS), funded by national as well as small specialist publications, uses social class categories such as ABCDE (see Table 2).

Table 2
Social class.

A	Professionals such as doctors, lawyers and dentists, chartered architects and engineers. Individuals with a large degree of responsibility such as senior executives and senior managers, higher grade civil servants and higher ranks of the armed services.
B	University lecturers, heads of local government departments, executive officers of the civil service, middle managers, qualified scientists, bank managers, police inspectors and senior ranks of the armed services.
C1	Nurses, technicians, pharmacists, salesmen, publicans, clerical workers, clerical officers within the civil service, police sergeants and constables and senior non-commissioned officers within the armed services.
C2	Skilled manual workers who have served apprenticeships; foremen, manual workers with special qualifications such as long-distance lorry drivers, security officers and other non-commissioned officers within the armed services.
D	Semi-skilled and unskilled manual workers, including labourers and people serving apprenticeships; clerical assistants in the civil service, machine minders, farm labourers, laboratory assistants, postmen and all other members of the armed services.
E	Pensioners, casual workers, long-term unemployed people, and others with relatively low or fixed levels of income.

Visual language is often international. You may not be able to read the newspapers here, but given your knowledge of the visual codes in your own country, you could easily guess the sort of publications these are, and their intended audience. Is tabloid design 'bad' design?

Communication

Introduction
Communication as a process
Semiotics
All design is political: part one
Afterword

The ABC system has its strengths but who's to say the people here (who you probably judged based on what they're wearing – see chapter 2) don't all share a secret obsession with boy bands, or have a love of rock climbing? A system that recognises shared values and lifestyles goes some way towards addressing this problem.

Using systems like ABC categories is known as demographics and is still used widely. But there are obvious problems: according to demographics a college lecturer is in social group B, while her students are in social group E. This assumes a great deal of parity between the incomes of different lecturers on the one hand, and between different students on the other, whereas the reality is that there is a huge range of incomes within each group. It also assumes that lecturers are different people from their students, with different tastes in music, reading material and clothes. In many cases this may be true, but not in all. Targeting college lecturers by assuming they are the same people as bank managers and senior police officers might prove to be a mistake. Another obvious problem is that pensioners, while stereotypically being seen as poor and infirm are increasingly wealthy and youthful. The system is so generalised that it ceases to be particularly useful, certainly for designers trying to communicate with groups of people.

Demographic systems have their uses, but they are too broad for many purposes. Recently marketers have turned to the idea that it is not so much what people do or how much they earn that determines their response to a message, but their attitude. Whereas demographics lump people together based on job, race and income, it is increasingly obvious that attitudes cross such boundaries. Defining your audience along purely demographic lines risks missing this, and so attitudinal means are required.

One system developed in the USA is known as Values and Lifestyles (VALS). This focuses more on what people want to achieve and the role they want to play in society. Table 3 shows the VALS2 system[12], which takes into account the fact that many people might aspire to certain values, but lack the financial or social ability to achieve them.

Other methods for categorising audiences include choice of magazine and newspaper, favourite television programmes, region, and even postal district – the idea that people tend to live near those who share the same attitudes and lifestyles is one adopted by producers of direct marketing (or 'junk mail' as it is more commonly known); putting your postcode into a 'geodemographic' database will return information such as the average car ownership, income, preferred holiday destination, satellite/cable television usage, and even the number of microwave ovens in use in your street[13].

Shannon and Weaver's process model of communication ignores issues such as social effects, politics, attitude and affluence of the message's receiver, but these things have a profound effect on the way any message will be understood.

Table 3 VALS2 categories.	Actualisers	Successful individuals
		Great deal of money
		Image is seen as a reflector of taste and character, not of power or status
		Interested in social issues
		Amenable to change
	Fulfilleds	Practical
		Value functionality and durability
		Mature, financially comfortable
		Satisfied with lives and situations
		Open to social change
	Achievers	Career-oriented
		Value stability and structure, self-discovery, intimacy
		Purchases gain image reflecting their success
	Experiencers	Love to spend
		Young, impulsive, enthusiastic
		Willing to try new things and take risks
	Believers	Highly principled, conservative consumers
		Purchase well-known brands
		Similar to fulfilleds but with less money
	Strivers	Like achievers, less well off
		Concerned about opinions of others, desire approval
	Makers	Like experiencers
		Active, self-sufficient
	Strugglers	Have to struggle to make ends meet

12
Taken from *Ads, Fads and Consumer Culture: Advertising's Impact on American Character and Society* by Arthur Asa Berger (Oxford: Rowman and Littlefield, 2000). See this book for a fuller description of other methods of categorising audiences including by postcode and magazine preference.

13
In the UK this system is known commercially as ACORN (www.caci.co.uk/acorn). At the time of writing, UK readers could check their neighbourhood's ACORN profile at www.upmystreet.com.

Using attitudes in the design process

Designers can use attitudinal systems like this to decide on a style or approach. A graphic designer asked to produce material for a bank might easily flounder without knowing who the audience is. If the client is targeting 'fulfilleds' the resulting design might be one that emphasises a comfortable retirement, happy children or grandchildren, or an expensive holiday. If, on the other hand, the target audience are 'strivers' then the design may emphasise access to a modest, but socially acceptable lifestyle using images of families in comfortable living rooms and kitchens, or driving a stylish but practical car. It's very easy to look at the designs around us and criticise them for being unsophisticated, or unchallenging – but visual language is like any other sort of language: there's no point speaking French to someone who only speaks English. Knowing your audience involves deciding on the correct visual language.

Attitudinal categories and audience profiles should not be used prescriptively, but can be a tool to spark creative thought – particularly when deadlines are looming.

Communication

Introduction
Communication as a process
Semiotics
All design is political: part one
Afterword

Noise, redundancy and entropy

Noise

So far we have ignored an important part of the process model; anything that gets added to the signal between sender and receiver is known as 'noise'. In technical terms level A noise is an obvious problem (smudged printing, bad workmanship, poor reception etc.), but it also exists in levels B and C as well. Level C (effectiveness) noise can occur if a message or product is hard to pick out among lots of others. The fact that a large number of people are doing other things while shopping or watching TV adds to the noise – even the type of chair you sit in or whether your feet ache has an effect[14].

At the semantic level (level B), noise can be caused by the receiver's cultural background (e.g. social, economic or ethnic) as well as by their social group (peer or family influences, for example). Problems particularly occur if the receiver misunderstands the codes used by the designer, or the message is hidden beneath too much decoration or unnecessary effect.

Visual communication and modernism

The concept of noise is not new as far as design is concerned. Around 1880 the British Arts and Crafts Movement reacted against the overly decorative styles that had become fashionable, calling instead for an aesthetic style of 'form follows function'. Its work was sometimes still highly decorative, but often quite plain while still being beautiful, revelling as it did in the materials being used.

The Arts and Crafts Movement in turn partly inspired the modernist aesthetic, which was mostly centred on Vienna in the 1920s and the Bauhaus in Weimar, Dessau and finally Berlin in the 1930s. This took the concept of form following function to new extremes and is famed for its often brutal paring down of everything from chairs and desk lamps to houses and office buildings.

Modernism proves that we can be effective without decoration; but it also shows we can go too far – the often resulting minimalism is sometimes only appreciated by a few 'visually educated' people and impoverished schemes have often meant it is conversely linked to socially ruinous housing schemes and ugly office complexes.

Too much decoration may be aesthetic noise, but decoration can also be the 'redundancy' that visual communication needs. This is arguably what the 'form follows function' maxim says – if the purpose is to communicate then the aesthetic language should support that, not detract from it.

14
A study of television viewing habits in the UK showed a range of diversions from chatting, reading and knitting through to kissing and even sex. It would take a very important message to interrupt some of these activities.

15
Sometimes known as 'Telephones' the game of Chinese Whispers involves somebody whispering a message into someone's ear. That person then whispers the message into another person's ear and so on until the last person announces the message to the whole group. The message is usually distorted, often amusingly, as we try to make sense of what we think we've heard. It's actually a really good model for the way communication works.

16
Newspapers often remove 'redundant' words from their headlines to fit them on the page. Sometimes the headlines still make sense, but sometimes it can be difficult to work out what they mean.

17
For a discussion of 'visual rhetoric' see the final chapter of *Advertising as Communication* by Gillian Dyer (London: Routledge, 1982).

The pursuit of poorly-funded modernist visions of housing led to a distrust of architecture and design that persists today. Estates like this often led to social problems rather than solved them. Ironically, those that haven't been demolished are becoming desirable residences for the affluent and trendy – postmodern in every sense.

Redundancy

About half the words in the English language are redundant – we could get away without using them and still make some sort of sense, but 'some sort' of sense is not always good enough. Shannon and Weaver were interested in this because they wanted to know how simple a message could be made, and how far it could be compressed, before it stopped making sense. A message can be compressed by being less wordy or using metaphors, and as far as telephones and radio are concerned the fidelity of the signal can be extremely low yet still understandable (compare the sound you hear on the telephone with a digital CD recording).

But if you think of communication as a game of Chinese Whispers[15], it becomes clear that even simple messages easily become distorted. The title 'Star Wars' often comes out completely differently despite its obvious simplicity and high recognition factor, but the phrase 'the popular science fiction film Star Wars' is more likely to survive intact, because the redundant part gives the important information (the title) a vital context. If somebody rattles off a series of numbers or colours at you, you will find it difficult to remember them. But if they preface the series with redundant phrases like 'my telephone number is' or 'the colours of the rainbow are' then things become easier. Redundancy adds context and aids understanding, and offers a sort of 'error check' so that if we don't quite hear one word we can fill in based on those we do hear[16].

If a design is intended to have a certain effect, be accessible or popular, process theory suggests that it needs to be highly redundant. This does not mean it cannot be creative. Many messages we send and receive are complex, but they can be made easier to understand by the use of redundancy and visual rhetoric such as metaphor, analogy, anecdote or clichés[17]. A lot of advertising places products in domestic settings to get around the complexity of the object being sold. Showing two happy children using their home computer with a smiling parent looking on while holding a school report with an 'A+' on it is a very quick way of getting across to the target audience the idea that buying a computer for your children will improve your life, and theirs, greatly – far better than attempting to explain processor speeds, graphics cards and other technical details.

The opposite of redundancy is entropy, and a highly entropic piece of communication might be one that uses technical language (such as a scientific paper, or a computer ad in a specialist magazine rather than a consumer one, as in the previous example) or an unfamiliar visual language. However, as entropic communication becomes familiar, it becomes redundant. Pickled sharks may once have been shocking when displayed in an art gallery, but today their shock value is questionable. As we will see in chapter 3, many designers advocate entropy in the creation of a constantly changing visual language. The danger of this, according to process theory, is that messages encoded in such ways will only be understood by a few people – which as Neville Brody points out, may be exactly your intention. But if you look around you it will be clear that most forms of communication, visual or otherwise, are marked by their high degree of redundancy. It is, in some senses, the grease that allows communication to run smoothly.

Communication

Introduction
Communication as a process
Semiotics
All design is political: part one
Afterword

Semiotics

The problem with the process model

18
There are two traditions of
semiotics, both developed
separately and simultaneously.
The first, credited to the
Swiss academic Ferdinand
de Saussure, sees semiotics
as a structure (hence the
term 'structuralism'), while
the American Charles Peirce
(pronounced 'purse') saw
semiotics as a social process.
The two views are not
incompatible, but it is the
Peircian view that informs the
discussion here. European
readers may be more familiar
with structuralism.

Models like Shannon and Weaver's
see communication as a linear
process with the intention of passing
a message from A to B. In this sense,
meaning is produced before it gets
to the recipient. But another theory,
semiotics, suggests communication
is not a process where meaning passes
from one point to another, but the
production of meaning itself. That's
not an easy concept to grasp at first
but it should become clearer later.

Visual communications and visual
culture are relatively new areas of study.
In the past, 'theory' of art and design
has concentrated on technical aspects
such as grids, typography, golden
sections, colour, the printing process,
weaving and so on. But critical theory,
which looks at the semantic and
effectiveness levels of design, has had
to be borrowed from other disciplines
such as history and sociology. These
theories don't offer rules, but observations
of how things work. Semiotics started
life as a means of studying linguistics[18]
and attempts to explain how we
communicate verbally by attaching
meanings arbitrarily to words. For
example, there's no reason why 'dog'
means 'four-legged furry creature'
because if it did, why is it other languages
use other words for the same thing?
The link between the word dog and
the thing is completely arbitrary. If that's
the first time you've ever come across
this concept you may think 'so what?' –
and I don't blame you. But once you
get past the seemingly pointless
aspect of semiotics, it soon becomes
an important and profound part of
visual communication.

Because it comes to us via linguistics
and literary studies a lot of the terms
take some getting used to, but it is
important that we start to adopt them.
A design (whether a chair, a dress or
a CD cover) is often known as a 'text'
and the person buying it, looking
at it, or using it is known as a 'reader'.
This implies then that there is an
'author', something we shall return
to throughout the book.

Rather than delve into the theory of
semiotics let's look first at some
examples of how it relates to visual
communications – we will unpick
the theory later.

Semiotics in practice

Flowers in themselves are completely meaningless, but they acquire one of several possible meanings when they are used as a sign, depending on the circumstances. Love, congratulations, condolences, sorrow – all from the same bunch.

The basic concept of semiotics is easier to understand in practice: the colour red 'means' nothing. It is just reflected light within a particular wavelength. Contrary to what you might think, it does not mean 'danger' or 'stop'. If it did then you would avoid anyone wearing a red coat, or with red hair, or with red lip-gloss. However, when used in particular circumstances, red acquires these meanings – it is used in traffic lights and on warning signs. Yet these associations are arbitrary; traffic lights could be any colour and they would still convey the same meaning so long as everybody involved in the process understood the colours to mean such things. This is why it's difficult to break away from convention and another reason that clichés work: if you decided one day to design a 'creative' set of traffic lights or warning signs in pastel shades you might destroy any meaning that has already been established. Designers need to be aware of what things mean and subvert them only when there is an intended effect.

Red, however, can also mean embarrassment, health (rosy cheeks), anger, authority and sex (red light district). Similarly green can mean envy, illness, fertility and inexperience as well as 'go' or 'safe'. It all depends on context, including cultural context – some colours and symbols mean completely different things in different parts of the world.

A bunch of flowers is a good example of a change in meaning. If you were to give the same bunch of flowers to a relative, someone who's sick, a lover, a stranger or a good friend, it would have a different meaning each time – as far as you were concerned at least. But no matter what the meaning you had in mind, they may be 'read' in ways you did not intend – if you have ever had an awkward moment with a friend because an innocent remark or gesture has been misinterpreted, you will know what I mean.

That is because signs have two levels of meaning, the one intended (denotation) and the one that is understood (connotation). If all is well, denotation and connotation will be the same, but it is the idea that they may not be that makes semiotics so fascinating – and frightening[19].

19
When a message is interpreted in a way that was not intended by the sender, it is known as an 'aberrant reading'. For a long time this was thought to be an unintended outcome of communication, but the Italian academic and author Umberto Eco suggests that because meaning is determined in large part by social aspects (race, gender, class etc.) then if the reader has a different social background from the author, the decoding of the message will be aberrant – and as this is very likely to happen in mass communications then aberrant readings must be the norm. This seemingly dry piece of theorising has profound implications for designers and anyone engaged in communications.

Certain colours and signs become visual shorthand over time. Energy drinks tend to display the same shape of can and a combination of blue, red and silver. Clichés are not a bad thing; trying to be 'original' risks confusing busy shoppers and confounding their expectations.

Communication

Semiotics in theory

Polysemy

Now for the theory: signs consist
of three elements:

Figure 4
A semiotic triangle. This diagram
has much in common with
Peirce's social conception of
semiotics and may be unfamiliar
if you have encountered the
structuralist model in the past.

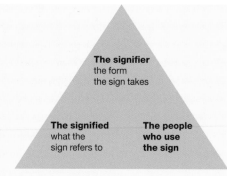

The signifier
the form
the sign takes

The signified
what the
sign refers to

**The people
who use
the sign**

There are three requirements
a sign must fulfil:

01
The signifier (the form of the sign) has
to be a thing and not a concept – so the
spoken or written word 'love' is a signifier,
but the concept it refers to is not. This
is not easy to understand at first so
a signifier is often described as a 'physical
object' that includes sounds and letters.
Things you can touch like clothes or
appliances, or visual marks like logos
and drawings are signifiers.

02
It has to refer to (or signify) something
other than itself – a bunch of flowers
or the colour red are not signs in
themselves unless they are used to refer
to love, danger and so on. In other
words the concept the signifier refers
to is what is being 'signified'.

03
Finally the signifier has to be understood
to refer to the signified by all those who
use it to communicate. This is often
socially or culturally specific, and signs
are part of the codes that society uses
to communicate.

Another important concept for visual
communication is the idea of 'polysemy'
or 'many meanings'. Put very simply, the
French writer Roland Barthes suggested
that all images are polysemous –
that is, they have more than one meaning.
Take a look at the image of the house
opposite and describe what you think
it means. You will probably find that
the meaning changes as you think about
it, and that as you think up a new meaning,
others occur to you (what Barthes calls
a 'chain of signifiers', as one meaning
is uncovered it leads to more). An image
is an 'open text'.

On page 39 you will see the same
image of the house with different text
attached. The same image now means
completely different things, but (and this
was Barthes's point) text fixes meaning.
The moment you add text to an image
you make it 'closed', no longer open to
interpretation.

Now consider the first set of symbols
at the top of the opposite page and
ask yourself what they mean. In an
experiment, several people applied
the meanings 'love', 'friendship', 'brother
and sister', and 'separation' to them –
completely different interpretations,
perhaps dependent on their own personal
circumstances at the time.

In fact the intended message was
simply 'male and female' – for which
a far better pair of signs is seen below.
The recipients added meaning to
the images that weren't intended by
the sender.

above
Often signs can be interpreted depending on not only the immediate context, but on the experiences of those interpreting them. The symbols at the top were variously interpreted as 'love' and 'separation' because of things that were happening in the interpreters' lives at the time. The biological symbols, on the other hand, seem to be devoid of this sort of contextual interpretation. When signs represent concepts (such as gender roles and values as here), they are said to be ideological and this makes them extremely powerful.

Communication

Introduction
Communication as a process
Semiotics
All design is political: part one
Afterword

opposite
When text is added to an image,
the endless possibilities of its
meaning are fixed so that just
one is possible (or at least, most
likely). In these examples, the
same image changes variously
from being somewhat threatening
to rather welcoming. Polysemy
can be useful if you deliberately
want an image to be ambiguous.

The death of the author

Earlier we mentioned that designs are referred to in semiotics as 'texts' and users of design as 'readers'. So where is the author in all this?

On the face of it, there could be two authors – the client (who owns the message) or the designer (who creates the design). The way design is taught often promotes the designer as the author, which leads to a shock for new designers the first time they deal with a client or art director who restricts them to a predetermined set of ideas or styles. Recently this conflict has led to a debate, particularly in graphic design, about authorship. Designers trained in the art tradition often see themselves as artists expressing themselves and perhaps ignore the needs of the client or the audience, claiming that 'the designer knows best'.

The debate ignores an important aspect of semiotic theory that has been alluded to in this chapter. The process model mentions noise as a possible distorter of a message and includes factors such as the environment, peer pressure, cultural background and even the type of chair a recipient is using, or the mood they're in. Semiotics too acknowledges the potential for aberrant reading, suggesting that it is the norm rather than the exception. In other words, meaning is created at the moment a text is read, not when it is written, which is what I meant when I said semiotics sees communication not as a process, but as the production of meaning. To put it simply, the reader is the author.

Roland Barthes coined the term 'the death of the author'[20] and it is an important point, because it changes the centre of gravity in the whole communication process. Whether you see the designer as being the facilitator of communication or the romantic artist struggling to express themselves and their inner turmoil, nothing counts more than what the reader understands and does with the design. As we shall see in chapter 2, the moment someone adds an accessory to a piece of clothing or modifies it in some way, draws doodles on a carefully designed magazine or uses it to empty the cat litter tray, or positions a hand-crafted cabinet in a room full of MDF reproductions, then the meaning changes.

This discussion of semiotics has been quite brief so far, but I want to move away from theory to practice. In the next chapter we will look at how semiotics works socially and culturally[21].

20
See chapter 3 for more on the death of the author.

21
For more on semiotics as it relates to design, see *Visible Signs* by David Crow (Lausanne, Switzerland: AVA Publishing SA, 2004). *An Introduction to Cultural Theory and Popular Culture* by John Storey (London: Prentice Hall, 1993) contains a useful discussion of semiotics and structuralism, while *Semiotics: The Basics* by Daniel Chandler (London: Routledge, 2002) is a thorough and accessible study of the whole area.

Don't talk to strangers

Peepshow

Traveller's rest

Safety and security

Come home to a warm welcome

The death of the author

Communication

All design is political: part one

Both the process and economic models described earlier acknowledge that when a design is commissioned it has the intention of conveying the commissioner's 'message'.

This is quite an easy concept to understand for graphic or information design, but how does the idea of visual communication fit into other disciplines such as fashion, product design, architecture, craft and so on? Surely there is no 'meaning' to convey here? In fact these ideas are relevant to all areas of design – and because it is less obvious it becomes even more important to understand.

Most, if not all, design is initiated to express a particular 'world view'. When a chain store orders a new range of clothes from a designer for the coming autumn season they are creating an idea (or message) about how they think people should look, and setting themselves up as the providers of that look. This is true whether the designer is being directed by the chain's visual manager or being given apparent autonomy. The ultimate aim of the chain is to sell lots of clothes and make money. As such their message competes with messages from rivals.

While it may seem that the winner is the outlet that meets the needs of consumers this is too risky a strategy, and so the whole process is wrapped up not just in finding out what people want but, importantly, in telling people what they want. The idea is to impose your world view on others and get them to (quite literally) buy into it.

The same is true of all seemingly meaningless designs such as furniture, wallpaper, even houses and office buildings.

Seen in this way it is clear that design serves to communicate the world view of the initiator (even in the case of non-commercial design where the world view is one of self-sufficiency, world peace or social justice). In other words, all design is 'political'.

We are starting to skirt around an important concept here that is actually central to the whole book, and to the study of communications and culture: ideology.

Are fashion-conscious people making a point about their cultural awareness, or are they simply pawns in a system that promotes constant consumption for other people's profit? Who tells us what to wear, how to behave, what to eat? Is western culture damaging indigenous cultures in the name of business? Are the plethora of fashion chains and brands providing consumer choice, or is the message – and the style – really just the same, dictated by a small group of people? Chapter 2 offers some answers.

Ideology – them and us

Karl Marx and visual communication

Karl Marx (1818–1883). Largely ignored in his lifetime, his wide-ranging ideas have gained increasing influence on areas as diverse as politics, sociology, cultural studies and economics. Often misrepresented and bent to suit political ideologies, his theories and those stemming from them offer useful insights into the way the world works.

22
For a good overview of the development of the word's meaning, see *New Keywords: A Revised Vocabulary of Culture and Society* by Tony Bennett, et al. (Oxford: Blackwell Publishing, 2005).

23
The connotations of Marxism are unfortunate as they immediately predispose a lot of people to reject anything labelled 'Marxist'. Many of the theorists discussed in this book can be called 'neo-Marxists' as they advance the original theories.

24
This is the 'political economy of the sign' – more on this in chapter 3.

Although the word 'ideology' has different meanings in different contexts[22], here it is quite specific and has its roots in classical Marxism. Karl Marx is a name that tends to be linked in people's minds with communism and extreme political views[23], so it might come as a surprise to read his name in a book on visual communications. But Marx's ideas, and more recent developments of them, are a central component of communication and cultural studies because they give us a theoretical framework in which to analyse the way people interact and live. If you pursue this field in any depth you will encounter Marx and his legacy time after time.

For Marxism, ideology is the process by which the ideas and world views of the dominant social groups come to be accepted as true. Everybody else operates within an economic and social system that serves the purposes of those groups and maintains their dominance. Our conscious image of who we are and how we relate to the world is unnatural (or a 'false consciousness' as Marx puts it) because it is determined not through nature or psychology, but by the manufactured world in which we live. We can link semiotics and the process model of communication here: signs become ideological when they stop operating in the semantic level of communication, and start to communicate in the conceptual and effectual level – meaning concepts like 'love' contained in commercially created events such as St Valentine's Day, the 'fight for peace', and the constant drive for 'family values' rather than more concrete instructions such as 'stop' or 'go'.

We are fed an image of how we should act or look by the visual images and objects around us, which are produced by those with access to the means of communication: newspaper proprietors, fashion houses, furniture retailers, governments, broadcasters and so on. Objects acquire a different set of values from their purely functional or economical ones (or 'use value' and 'exchange value') and possess a new value as either a gift or a status symbol[24]. We are driven to seek happiness not by acquiring things that are useful, but by surrounding ourselves with signs that we are fulfilled. This is a situation perpetuated by the people who produce the objects (for whom they retain their simple use and exchange values) by adding meaning in the way they are advertised or shown in style magazines and celebrity features.

So the communication process is an ideological process, and design is an agent of ideology in that it communicates (for good or bad) the political intentions of the person or organisation that commissions it. We will look at counter-arguments to this rather depressing view in the next two chapters.

Communication

Introduction
Communication as a process
Semiotics
All design is political: part one
Afterword

Afterword

No more rules?

25
See *Introduction to Communication Studies* by John Fiske (London: Routledge, 1990) for more on the different theories of communication.

26
Dictionary of Communication and Media Studies by James Watson and Anne Hill (London: Hodder Arnold, 2003).

I said at the start of this chapter that communication theory doesn't claim to be anything more than theory, and what's been presented here is only a small part of a huge discipline. Indeed, the Shannon and Weaver model has been superseded many times – the reason it has been discussed here is because it is simple and fits the design process quite neatly. It isn't the end of the story, however. In one dictionary of media and communications[25] I counted over 20 quite different models, but that communications can be modelled in some way is in itself quite profound and challenging.

Theories help us to understand how things work. But the response of some designers to theory, that it is something to be avoided or subverted, is puzzling. Reactions later in this chapter could be said to fall into this category because they claim theory restricts creativity[26] by telling designers what typefaces or colours to use, or whether text should be centred on a page or not. But none of the theories discussed in this book says anything of the sort.

In the same way that the theory of gravity explains why planets orbit the sun, but doesn't say that they all have to look the same, so communication theory only attempts to explain how communication works, and what causes it not to work. From this, a set of guiding principles can be determined but they are only guides. If a design works, it works; communication theory can help us explain why but it never goes so far as to present a set of rules about what things should look like. What the theory tells us, however, is that the final arbiter of what works or not is the reader, the audience, the buyer – not the designer, the critic or the client. Perhaps it is this that worries people; it is something we return to in the final chapter.

I don't see theory as the iron cage some designers claim it to be. If you step outside any cage you'll see a framework, something to support and give structure to whatever is built around it. And just as five different architects will take the same plot of land, the same 'restrictions', the same theories and the same underlying structure, yet produce five completely different buildings, so communication theory helps rather than restricts creativity. Take the structure away and you're left with a house of cards, ready to fall at the slightest critical touch.

In this chapter we looked at:

Shannon and Weaver's description of communication as a process.

Three types of problem in communication: technical, semantic and effectiveness.

The relationship between the client, the designer and the audience. Who is in charge of the message being communicated?

Ways of describing audiences, both in terms of the social and financial background, and their shared values and lifestyles.

The roles played by noise, redundancy and entropy in communication: noise being anything that interferes with the clear communication of the message; redundancy being the elements that are unnecessary, but that help ensure clarity; and entropy being the opposite of redundancy – a feature of messages that are plainly articulated, but difficult to understand.

Semiotics: the idea that meanings are attached arbitrarily to words and images through shared understandings.

The role of cliché as an important means of ensuring expedient communication.

The three elements that go towards the production of signs: an object, word or image; something that it represents; and the people who share the same interpretation of it.

Polysemy: in particular, the idea that images contain a chain of meanings, but that the meaning is fixed when text is applied.

Authorship: we revisited the idea that the client or, in some cases, the designer, is the author of meaning. Given the ideas surrounding semiotics it is clear that meaning is often out of the control of anyone – except perhaps the reader who is free to interpret (or misinterpret) the message as much as he or she wants.

Finally, we looked at the idea that all design has an ideological purpose (innocent or otherwise), which makes it vitally important to understand how it works. Studying design is more than being able to 'do' it; it is about 'being' a designer and understanding the responsibilities and power that come with the role.

The Practice

Introduction

Chapter 1 at first appears to be setting out indisputable facts about the theory of communication, but it is actually asking us to consider what graphic designers do and why. Your interpretation of the theoretical text will identify an allegiance to a design camp. Although it isn't full-scale war, be warned – once you put your head over this particular parapet you risk being shot at.

Opposing views are often expressed in the graphic design press. These tend to be articulated less through debates about aesthetics and more about communication. Whose message are we communicating? How evident should the designer be in this process? How do we indicate by our work the importance we place on graphic design? For the passionate and committed, graphic design is less a way of earning a living and more a justification of life itself. Where a designer positions him- or herself in relation to communication is an indicator of a whole design philosophy, as our two practitioners will reveal.

Consider this simple observation. A Mac operator in a high street print shop also offers a graphic design service. This places graphic design in the realms of a trade or craft. A client needs a letterhead, so goes to a print shop; they do some layouts, the client selects one design and the shop prints it.

Job done. No soul-searching for a concept, no agonising about proportion, colour, font choice or size, no justification of design principles. Does the letterhead work? Well, you can put a letter on it and send it in the post. It is all spelt correctly and the client is happy that it communicates something. It feels right. But from a professional designer's point of view it is conventional and unsophisticated and unless considered ironically it shouldn't be allowed to cast its shadow on the graphic design world. But it does communicate on a basic level and subliminally on other levels too.

What does this reveal? That the practice of graphic design is not adequately defined perhaps? What is it that makes this person moving type around on a letterhead less a designer and more a technician? It is not only about the marks on the page, it is about the thinking that puts them there. For some, this is about applying theories to govern the process, while others question the realm of a designer's influence and responsibility. 'Professional' designers have wildly differing ideas of what they are there to do, but the defining question is about communication. What? Why? How? To whom? In considering the communication process we are halfway to determining what a designer is, might or should be.

The practitioners

The two practitioners commentating on chapter 1 are both graphic designers: Neville Brody and Michael Bierut. Given the subject of this chapter, it was important to discuss it with graphic designers who speak with a great deal of experience. They are engaged and passionate practitioners with a degree of objectivity and an understanding of the multifarious expectations of clients and end-users alike.

Initially, Brody worked in record-cover design, but he made his name largely through his experimental work as art director of *Face* magazine. Brody was one of the first 'star' graphic designers. In 1988, the first of two monographs of Brody's work was published and an accompanying exhibition of his work was held at the Victoria & Albert Museum in London, which subsequently toured Europe and Japan. This experience could have removed him totally from everyday practice, but since shooting to celebrity status in the 1980s he has also weathered some storms and it is this combined experience that makes him a perfect commentator for this chapter.

In the mid-1990s Brody and his business partner launched Research Studios, a small London-based design studio working internationally across all media. From his student days to the present, Brody has challenged perceived notions of 'good' design. He is unabashed in his belief in the designer's voice. Despite his high profile Brody might be seen to have positioned himself on the periphery of the design establishment, perceiving himself as more radical and alternative.

Michael Bierut is an objective and intelligent commentator on the design world, while also being embedded in the design establishment. He has won many design awards; his work is represented in the permanent collections of several internationally renowned museums; he has served as president of the New York Chapter of the American Institute of Graphic Arts and as a member of the Alliance Graphique Internationale, a global community of graphic designers. Would this give him a more or less pragmatic approach to the process of design?

After working at Vignelli Associates for ten years Bierut joined Pentagram in New York as a partner. Pentagram's structure is unusual for an international design consultancy. Each partner runs their own autonomous group, which means that the support of a larger organisation is available while giving partners the creative and hands-on benefits of a smaller and more intimate set up, including more direct client contact and answerability.

Both Brody and Bierut have worked for multinational corporations as much as for small independent organisations. Both also initiate projects that are centred on the design process. Through his company Research Publishing, Brody has for ten years produced Fuse, a forum for experimental typography. Bierut meanwhile has knowledge, interest and expertise that is particularly pertinent to this book, having co-edited the series *Looking Closer: Critical Writings on Graphic Design*.

Neville Brody

Biography

Neville Brody was born in London in 1957, and studied graphic design at the London College of Printing, graduating in 1979.

Brody has been at the forefront of graphic design for over two decades. His work has encompassed almost every area of graphic design, from designing record covers to magazines.

In 1988, the first of two monographs of Brody's work was published, which became the world's best-selling graphic design book. An accompanying exhibition of his work at the Victoria & Albert Museum in London attracted over 40,000 visitors before touring Europe and Japan.

In 1994, together with partner Fwa Richards, Brody launched Research Studios, a London-based design studio. Partner studios have recently opened in Paris and Berlin, with plans to imminently open in New York. Research Studios works across all media, from web to print, and from environmental and retail design to moving graphics and film titles.

A sister company, Research Publishing, produces and publishes experimental multimedia works by young artists. The primary focus is Fuse, the renowned conference and forum for experimental typography and communications. The publication is approaching its twentieth issue, over a publishing period of more than ten years. Three Fuse conferences have so far been held in London, San Francisco and Berlin.

Brody has designed many successful websites, including Guardian Unlimited, Britain's most popular newspaper website, and art-directed international magazine titles, including *Arena*, *City Limits*, *Lei*, *Per Lui* and *Actuel*.

Research Studio's client list features branding and special projects for the following clients: Express, Kenzo, Issey Miyake, Macromedia, Sony, Pepsi, Warner, Paramount, Disney, Channel 4, adidas-Salomon, Nike, ORF, TF1, Gaultier, Guerlain, Armani, Yves Saint Laurent, BBC, Royal Court Theatre, ICA and Ricoh.

Brody exploits the possibilities of typographic form in his work and often utilises experimental typefaces as the basis of a design.

left to right, top to bottom
Leaflet cover for Made in Clerkenwell open studios, 2003, based on a typeface by Research Studios designer Jeff Knowles; book for the Paris Olympic Landmark competition, 2004; exhibition guide for Art in Sacred Spaces, 2000, in which 'sacred' and 'spaces' intersect to create new forms; Interact 1, 2004, exhibition invitation; *Macromedia Using Freehand 9*, 1995, manual cover.

CONCOURS INTERNATIONAL D'ARCHITECTURE POUR LA RÉALISATION DU REPÈRE OLYMPIQUE, PARIS, FRANCE

INTERNATIONAL ARCHITECTURE COMPETITION FOR THE RÉALISATION OF THE OLYMPIC LANDMARK, PARIS, FRANCE

454 PROJETS POUR PARIS 2012 454 PROJECTS FOR PARIS 2012

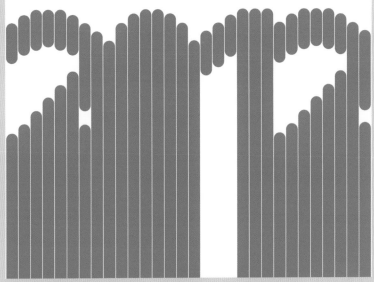

left to right
This packaging was for
Fuse 1, Invention, 1991.
A renowned platform for
experimental typography.

Fuse involves regular conferences
and a quarterly publication
of specially designed typefaces
and posters in response to
a central theme, as in Fuse 17,
Echo, 2000 (posters by Ann-Lisa
Schönecker, Florian Heiss,
Function, Pierre di Sciullo and
Neville Brody).

Brody read chapter 1 thoroughly and expressed some frustration with parts of the text. As we talked it became apparent that this was much of what he had rejected as a student at the London College of Printing – that there is a wrong and a right way to design: '...they taught that design should be objective, so we were told there were specific rules, the kinds of colour you should use, whether stuff should be ranged left or centred, whether it's serif or sans serif... I was at college at the time of punk and my biggest influences at the time were Dadaism and Constructivism. The message for me from that work was that actually anything is possible.'

For Brody it is impossible to apply the same means of assessment to all pieces of design. Work succeeds or fails according to differing criteria. All this is determined by the brief. Mass communication, for example, is not always an objective. '[To set text reading] left to right is a decision to make it more globally accessible. You may decide to do it the other way around, in which case you know that you'll only have one per cent of people who get it or attempt it – but that might be your goal.'

Brody was taught by practitioners who advocated the designer taking a position of neutrality in communication between client and end-user. This is a modernist position. It is about transparency, increased access, clarity of purpose revealed through limited means. This may have resulted in a minimalist aesthetic but it was never merely a 'style'. This was an approach to life, to politics, to society. Brody embraced some aspects of modernism, as demonstrated by his interest in developing systematic solutions and belief in design for public service, but he considered objectivity impossible to achieve. 'I believed that design and advertising were manipulative,' Brody explains. 'I wanted to understand the core rules in order to turn them on their head and reveal this manipulative process. The philosophy of my work is always to reveal, not conceal.

'I felt it was key to reveal the involvement of the human hand in the process of delivering idea A to destination B. I was at college at the time when it was thought that designers should be seen and not heard, but this is a fallacy. Designers translate invisible concepts into tangible form. In the act of making it tangible we make it subjective. So certainly in all my early work the "noise" that's referred to in this chapter was made very, very apparent so that the reader would be very aware that someone had been involved in interpreting the idea.

'As Roland Barthes says, ultimately the reader is the author. That has been embodied in my work since the beginning. I've deliberately incorporated ambiguity into my work, I've deliberately not stated something as fact in my work, because I've recognised that the process of communication is a dialogue, not a monologue. I'm not dictating, I'm part of the message that I'm transporting. How could I be so arrogant as to assume I can tell the reader what they should think about what is being communicated? Authorship is a shared thing. We're producing works that are catalysts for thought, which are interpreted differently by every single person that looks at them.'

Brody considers the use of cliché as potentially 'preventing new thought', but cites Research Studio's recent promotional work for the Royal Court Theatre as an example of cliché used more inventively. 'The first show we worked on was about the inevitable fall and shame of a popular figure in entertainment. The writer and director wanted to use an image of a man falling on a banana skin. We thought this potentially corny and clichéd but used it as a jumping off point to producing a modern and relevant solution. The difficulty is that most clients prefer to be delivering clichés... it's not in the interests of advertising to make people think. It's in the interests of advertising to make people accept without being aware of the process.

'My role is to use my work to help awaken people's minds, not close them,' said Brody. This process of raising awareness can take many subtle forms. In taking on a job, a designer is generally agreeing to help a client communicate a message. From here, the designer effectively endorses the message, so the most important factor is to find the right clients with the right intended messages. 'Designers are "agents of ideology", it's indivisible from ideology,' Brody agrees.

It is undoubtedly true that communication is not a completely controllable process and that clients have to accept that a designer's choice of typeface can impact on the receipt of the message just as much as reader experience or expectation. Brody argues that the level and type of design intervention is determined by appropriateness.

'I deal with culture,' Brody went on to explain, 'which is often an exploratory space. It has very little to do with basic human needs even though it has a lot to do with psychological survival. If I were working for the voluntary sector or in health-related design I would concentrate largely in the area of storytelling and necessarily would not embellish it or create a degree of ambiguity. I would still try and inject an element of free-thinking into the space and I would still feel I had the right to question what the client was saying. Just because the client is in a righteous position it doesn't mean that what they believe in is gospel.'

Brody is clear that it is the brief, appropriateness and function that determine the outcome of any job. 'Form follows function is absolutely correct, but the modernists didn't come up with that notion, it was their definition of function that changed. The romantics followed the paradigm absolutely, but for them the function of visual communication was entirely different. The Bauhaus tried to establish a separation from romantic to mechanical. But giving or receiving love is a function. Entertainment is still a function. For something to sell – that can still be a function.'

Brody's experience of the technical level is that clients expect his input and advice. From format to paper choice or use of colour these choices are not predetermined by a client before he is involved. 'What is difficult is when a client says they want a poster and you propose a website,' adds Brody. 'Sometimes we end up having to do something that we don't support because it's part of a bigger process. I think compromise is valid provided there is a respect for the relevant skill set.'

Brody has worked internationally and can compare the level of respect clients from different countries afford the designer. 'The English client feels visually informed enough to make a judgement on the basis of assumed knowledge, which is bullshit because they're not trained. They just assume that because Britain is quite a visual society they have the ability to take the correct decision. Whereas when we work with German or Japanese clients they feel uninformed. They want to work with an established creative partner to bring skills that they don't have.'

Working with the fashion and cosmetics industry, Brody has found open-minded clients. These advertisements for Tribeca Issey Miyake, 2001, are for the company's worldwide flagship store and art space, and include a constructivist-style montage and customised font.

As with all designers, Brody has experienced a breakdown in effective communication between client and designer, which could have jeopardised a project long before it reached the end-user. He describes the identity work that Research Studios has recently completed for the Korean tyre firm Hankook.

'They came to us because they couldn't break into any other markets because their image was so bad. Our job was to apply global references to a local story. When we did that, they accused us of not having done our research and of not understanding their industry. It was probably the most painful process we've ever been through. The cultural divide was so big – for instance, our studio would close at 6 or 7 at night, whereas in Korea if you're not working until 11 at night you're showing disloyalty to the company. So we were being disloyal by going home at a reasonable time. To not complete the job could have meant bankruptcy for us and I believed in what we produced. They've applied it to everything now, very successfully, and there have been various reports of how it's helped to raise their profile, that it's allowed them to open markets.'

When it comes to the effectiveness question Brody, like most designers, mistrusts the focus group as something that has the semblance of objectivity but is actually easy to manipulate. 'You have to think about the kind of person that would agree to be in a focus group,' points out Brody. 'There's some self-validation need going on. We have never ever worked with a focus group. Some of our clients probably have, as part of the process, but we have never experienced a client coming back to us and saying they've done focus group testing and we need to change what we've done.'

Audience categorisation sounds horribly autocratic. This doesn't mean that designers should not consider their intended audience – far from it – but in keeping with his overall approach to design Brody questions the intention. 'We've never ever incorporated it,' he explains. 'I think we've been more instinctual. We agree more or less with the American "value-added-lifestyle" idea even though we don't follow it. It's much more cultural than the ABCs. People are obsessed with this need to categorise in order to control because the opposite is so terrifying.'

Does Brody ever refer to theoretical approaches in his discussions with clients? 'There's a pseudo-science that's attached to branding, and semiotic theories are necessary in the eyes of the client to understand the branding created for them.' But Brody feels that to apply the theory too knowingly can be another form of manipulation. 'I think semiotics is really useful as part of a process of understanding, but to apply it knowingly in order to manipulate the outcome of a piece of communication is cynicism.'

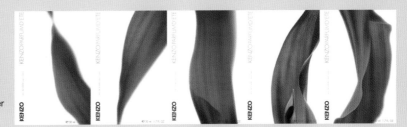

Since designing their website in 2000, Research Studios have redesigned all of Kenzo Perfume's packaging. For Kenzo Parfum d'été, 2003, five different versions of the design were presented to Kenzo, which decided to produce all of them and allow the consumer an opportunity for choice.

The theory of semiotics is correct. Brody explains: 'You might have a criterion that things should be legible. But legibility exists on a number of different levels. So, you can read "B loves A" but your choice of font will completely change the receipt of that message. This is semiotics. A choice of font is a sign.' However, Brody identifies a problem; meaning is subject to change. 'In China yellow means sickness or death. But then McDonald's is in China and they use yellow as a strong component. Does that very presence change the conception of yellow? At what point does the object actually change the sign or the signification?'

Brody's student experience has informed his whole working life. His concern with chapter 1 is that contemporary students might feel disheartened to see the process laid bare and reduced to something that sounds rather mechanical, and yet he also fears that students are not being given enough guidance anymore. 'Students are not being taught that rules even exist. They're basically taught within a vacuum. This has encouraged them to be original. I support originality as long as there is still a contextualising process that goes on, as long as there's guidance, but that doesn't exist.'

For Brody experimentation and pushing boundaries is valid and to be encouraged. He sees no problem with the pursuit of the 'original' or a spotlight falling on 'creativity', although this is always tempered by his approach to appropriateness and function. Is Brody not concerned that this encourages designer self-obsession and a detachment from the real world in which graphic design operates? He sees this as an inevitable, though troubling political legacy. 'Thatcher encouraged individual opportunism, and a unique voice is therefore encouraged as being very commercially viable.'

Brody is obviously worried by his own legacy and that of those like him. Tutors seem to have lost confidence since his generation tore down the design idyll, but nothing has replaced it. The result is a new generation of designers who can't lose their way because they haven't found one to lose. 'My tutors tried to throw me out... when they saw I'd succeeded, that I could actually not only get work as a designer but that I would become influential, they felt a total sense of confusion and failure. So their response was that the college stopped teaching students, and left them to their own devices. And that is a tradition that's still pretty apparent. It's completely wrong. Teachers are there to engage with the student, and help guide him or her on their own course. It's supposed to be a process of engagement. It's not stand off and it's not dictate... the role of the teacher is to try and contextualise or make redundant, according to this theory, the work that the student is doing.'

Cultural differences contributed to the difficulties in this project for Korean tyre manufacturers Hankook, 2003–04. Research Studios was asked to design a corporate identity programme that would help engineer growth and a more competitive profile for the struggling company.

Misunderstandings made this process painful for both designer and client, but the end product was ultimately successful in meeting the client's objectives.

These corporate identity guidelines provide instruction on the application and implementation of the programme, including the dynamic tyre-tread symbol, and the contemporary logotype that utilises upper and lower case, a bold sans serif font and italics to suggest technological sophistication, reliability and a world-class corporation.

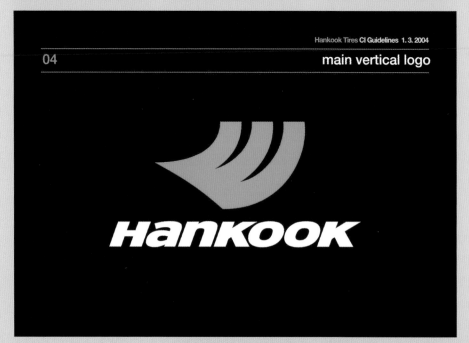

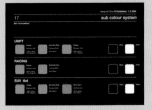

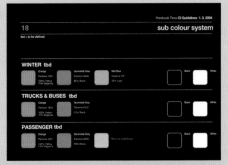

Font = Hankook Black Lower Case

Note : UHPT will have an independent logo

Brody sees the designer's role as helping to awaken the minds of both client and audience, but he is insistent that design intervention is determined by appropriateness and function.

Working with the Royal Court Theatre on its programme for Autumn, 2004, the client wanted to use the image of a man falling on a banana skin, a cliché Brody and his team chose to reinterpret rather than discard.

CALENDAR AUTUMN SEASON 2004

	TIME	JERWOOD THEATRE DOWNSTAIRS		TIME	JERWOOD THEATRE UPSTAIRS	
SEPT						
THU 2	19.30	DUMB SHOW	RES P			
FRI 3	19.30	DUMB SHOW	RES P			
SAT 4	19.30	DUMB SHOW	RES P			
MON 6	19.30	DUMB SHOW	P			
TUE 7	19.00	DUMB SHOW	PN			
WED 8	19.30	DUMB SHOW				
THU 9	19.30	DUMB SHOW			19.45	BONE	P
FRI 10	19.30	DUMB SHOW			19.45	BONE	P
SAT 11	15.30	DUMB SHOW				
	19.30	DUMB SHOW			19.45	BONE	P
MON 13	19.30	DUMB SHOW			19.00	BONE	PN
TUE 14	19.30	DUMB SHOW			19.00	BONE	PN
WED 15	19.30	DUMB SHOW			19.45	BONE	
THU 16	19.30	DUMB SHOW			19.45	BONE	
FRI 17	19.30	DUMB SHOW			19.45	BONE	
SAT 18	15.30	DUMB SHOW			16.00	BONE	
	19.30	DUMB SHOW			19.45	BONE	
MON 20	19.30	DUMB SHOW			19.45	BONE	
TUE 21	19.30	DUMB SHOW			19.45	BONE	SIP
WED 22	19.30	DUMB SHOW			19.45	BONE	
THU 23	19.30	DUMB SHOW			19.45	BONE	
FRI 24	19.30	DUMB SHOW			19.45	BONE	
SAT 25	15.30	DUMB SHOW			16.00	BONE	
	19.30	DUMB SHOW			19.45	BONE	
MON 27	19.30	DUMB SHOW				
TUE 28	19.30	DUMB SHOW	CAP			
WED 29	19.30	DUMB SHOW	T			
THU 30	14.30	DUMB SHOW	E			
	19.30	DUMB SHOW				
OCT						
FRI 1	19.30	DUMB SHOW			19.45	THE WEATHER	P
SAT 2	15.30	DUMB SHOW	AD			
	19.30	DUMB SHOW			19.45	THE WEATHER	P
MON 4	19.30	DUMB SHOW			19.45	THE WEATHER	P
TUE 5	19.00	DUMB SHOW			19.45	THE WEATHER	P
					21.30	BEAR HUG	P
WED 6	19.30	DUMB SHOW			19.45	THE WEATHER	P
					21.30	BEAR HUG	P
THU 7	15.30	DUMB SHOW				
	19.30	DUMB SHOW	SIP		19.45	THE WEATHER	P
					21.30	BEAR HUG	P
FRI 8	19.30	DUMB SHOW			19.00	THE WEATHER	PN
					20.45	BEAR HUG	PN
SAT 9	15.30	DUMB SHOW			16.00	THE WEATHER	
	19.30	DUMB SHOW			19.45	THE WEATHER	
					21.30	BEAR HUG	
MON 11					19.45	THE WEATHER	
					21.30	BEAR HUG	
TUE 12					19.45	THE WEATHER	G
					21.30	BEAR HUG	
WED 13					19.45	THE WEATHER	
					21.30	BEAR HUG	
THU 14					19.45	THE WEATHER	SIP
					21.30	BEAR HUG	SIP
FRI 15					19.45	THE WEATHER	
					15.30	BEAR HUG	
SAT 16					16.00	THE WEATHER	
					19.45	THE WEATHER	
					21.30	BEAR HUG	
MON 18	19.30	MORTIMER'S MISCELLANY			19.45	THE WEATHER	
TUE 19					19.45	THE WEATHER	
WED 20					14.30	THE WEATHER	E
					19.45	THE WEATHER	
THU 21					19.45	THE WEATHER	

	TIME	JERWOOD THEATRE DOWNSTAIRS		TIME	JERWOOD THEATRE UPSTAIRS	
FRI 22					19.45	THE WEATHER	
SAT 23					16.00	THE WEATHER	
					19.45	THE WEATHER	
MON 25					19.45	THE WEATHER	
TUE 26					19.45	THE WEATHER	
WED 27					19.45	THE WEATHER	
THU 28	19.30	FORTY WINKS	RES P		19.45	THE WEATHER	
FRI 29	19.30	FORTY WINKS	RES P		19.45	THE WEATHER	
SAT 30					16.00	THE WEATHER	
	19.30	FORTY WINKS	RES P		19.45	THE WEATHER	
NOV						
MON 1	19.30	FORTY WINKS	P			
TUE 2	19.30	FORTY WINKS	RES P			
WED 3	19.00	FORTY WINKS	PN			
THU 4	19.30	FORTY WINKS				
FRI 5	19.30	FORTY WINKS			19.45	FRESH KILLS	P
SAT 6	12.30	BUILDING TOUR				
	15.30	FORTY WINKS				
	19.30	FORTY WINKS			19.45	FRESH KILLS	P
MON 8	19.30	FORTY WINKS			19.00	FRESH KILLS	PN
TUE 9	19.30	FORTY WINKS			19.00	FRESH KILLS	PN
WED 10	19.30	FORTY WINKS	SIP		19.45	FRESH KILLS	
THU 11	19.30	FORTY WINKS	T		19.45	FRESH KILLS	
FRI 12	19.30	FORTY WINKS			19.45	FRESH KILLS	
SAT 13	15.30	FORTY WINKS			16.00	FRESH KILLS	
	19.30	FORTY WINKS			19.45	FRESH KILLS	
MON 15	19.30	FORTY WINKS			19.45	FRESH KILLS	
TUE 16	19.30	FORTY WINKS			19.45	FRESH KILLS	
WED 17	19.30	FORTY WINKS			19.45	FRESH KILLS	SIP
THU 18	19.30	FORTY WINKS			19.45	FRESH KILLS	
FRI 19	19.30	FORTY WINKS			19.45	FRESH KILLS	
SAT 20	15.30	FORTY WINKS			16.00	FRESH KILLS	
	19.30	FORTY WINKS			19.45	FRESH KILLS	
MON 22	19.30	FORTY WINKS				
TUE 23	19.30	FORTY WINKS				
WED 24	19.30	FORTY WINKS				
THU 25	19.30	FORTY WINKS				
FRI 26	19.30	FORTY WINKS			19.45	A GIRL IN A CAR WITH A MAN	P
SAT 27	15.30	FORTY WINKS				
	19.30	FORTY WINKS			19.45	A GIRL IN A CAR WITH A MAN	P
MON 29	19.30	FORTY WINKS			19.00	A GIRL IN A CAR WITH A MAN	PN
TUE 30	19.30	FORTY WINKS			19.00	A GIRL IN A CAR WITH A MAN	PN
DEC						
WED 1	19.30	FORTY WINKS			19.45	A GIRL IN A CAR WITH A MAN	
THU 2	15.30	FORTY WINKS				
					19.45	A GIRL IN A CAR WITH A MAN	
FRI 3	19.30	FORTY WINKS			19.45	A GIRL IN A CAR WITH A MAN	
SAT 4	15.30	FORTY WINKS			16.00	A GIRL IN A CAR WITH A MAN	
	19.30	FORTY WINKS			19.45	A GIRL IN A CAR WITH A MAN	
MON 6					19.45	A GIRL IN A CAR WITH A MAN	
TUE 7					19.45	A GIRL IN A CAR WITH A MAN	
WED 8					14.30	A GIRL IN A CAR WITH A MAN	E
					19.45	A GIRL IN A CAR WITH A MAN	SIP
THU 9					19.45	A GIRL IN A CAR WITH A MAN	
FRI 10					19.45	A GIRL IN A CAR WITH A MAN	
SAT 11					16.00	A GIRL IN A CAR WITH A MAN	
					19.45	A GIRL IN A CAR WITH A MAN	
MON 13					19.45	A GIRL IN A CAR WITH A MAN	
TUE 14					19.45	A GIRL IN A CAR WITH A MAN	
WED 15					19.45	A GIRL IN A CAR WITH A MAN	
THU 16					19.45	A GIRL IN A CAR WITH A MAN	
FRI 17					19.45	A GIRL IN A CAR WITH A MAN	
SAT 18					16.00	A GIRL IN A CAR WITH A MAN	
						A GIRL IN A CAR WITH A MAN	

ROYAL COURT

PN	PRESS NIGHT	T	POST-SHOW TALK
P	PREVIEW	SIP	SIGN-INTERPRETED PERFORMANCE
RES	RESIDENTS' OFFER	AD	AUDIO-DESCRIBED PERFORMANCE & TOUCH TOUR

CAP	CAPTIONED PERFORMANCE
E	EDUCATION MATINEE
G	GALA

THERE ARE NO PERFORMANCES ON SUNDAY

Research Studios' work for the
ICA has provided opportunities
for experimentation in both
design and production. The
inventive format of this catalogue
for the Beck's Futures 2003
exhibition includes an apparently
sun-bleached cardboard box
containing nine loose-leaf
A2 broadsheets, one for each
exhibiting artist. Inside each
folded broadsheet is stapled
an A6 text insert. The publication
resembles an artist's edition
and playfully manipulates the
associations and expectations of
the contemporary art audience.

Francis Upritchard
Save Yourself, 2002
Mummy-bandages, glass eye, hair, motor, CD player and canopic urns

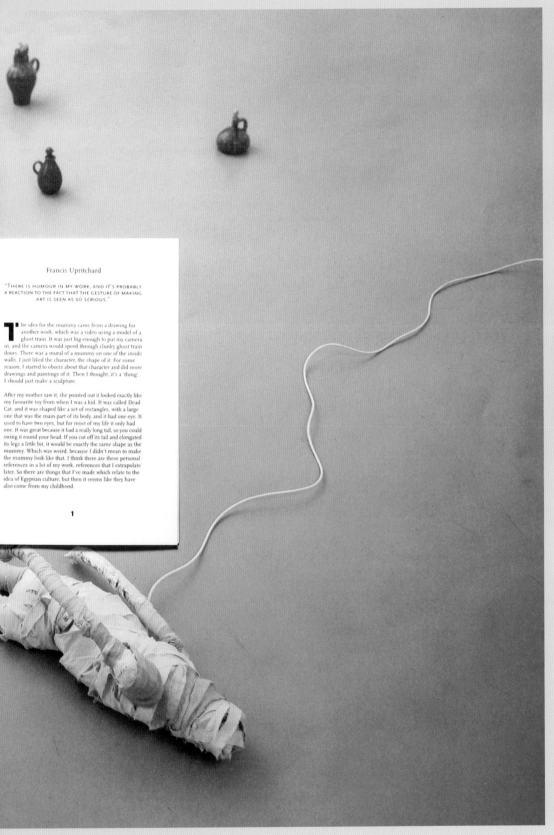

Francis Upritchard

"There is humour in my work, and it's probably a reaction to the fact that the gesture of making art is seen as so serious."

The idea for the mummy came from a drawing for another work, which was a video using a model of a ghost train. It was just big enough to put my camera in, and the camera would speed through clunky ghost train doors. There was a mural of a mummy on one of the inside walls. I just liked the character, the shape of it. For some reason, I started to obsess about that character and did more drawings and paintings of it. Then I thought, it's a 'thing', I should just make a sculpture.

After my mother saw it, she pointed out it looked exactly like my favourite toy from when I was a kid. It was called Dead Cat, and it was shaped like a set of rectangles, with a large one that was the main part of its body, and it had one eye. It used to have two eyes, but for most of my life it only had one. It was great because it had a really long tail, so you could swing it round your head. If you cut off its tail and elongated its legs a little bit, it would be exactly the same shape as the mummy. Which was weird, because I didn't mean to make the mummy look like that. I think there are these personal references in a lot of my work, references that I extrapolate later. So there are things that I've made which relate to the idea of Egyptian culture, but then it seems like they have also come from my childhood.

1

Michael Bierut

Biography

Michael Bierut was born in Cleveland, Ohio, USA, in 1957, and studied graphic design at the University of Cincinnati's College of Design, Architecture, Art and Planning. Prior to joining Pentagram in 1990 as a partner in the firm's New York office, he worked for ten years at Vignelli Associates, ultimately as vice-president of graphic design.

Pentagram is owned and run by a group of partners who are all working designers: graphic designers, product designers and architects. The 19 Pentagram partners head up their own groups of designers, each of which operates autonomously. Pentagram is currently one of the largest and most well-established design consultancies in the world, with five offices in Europe and America.

Bierut's clients at Pentagram have included The Council of Fashion Designers of America, The Minnesota Children's Museum, The Walt Disney Company, Mohawk Paper Mills, Motorola, Princeton University, the Brooklyn Academy of Music and the Library of Congress. His projects have ranged from the design of I Want to Take You Higher, an exhibition on the psychedelic era for the Rock and Roll Hall of Fame and Museum, to leading a team to redesign print graphics, interiors, product design and uniforms for United Airlines.

He has won many design awards and his work is represented in the permanent collections of the Museum of Modern Art and the Metropolitan Museum of Art in New York, and the Musée des Arts Décoratifs, Montreal. He served as president of the New York Chapter of the American Institute of Graphic Arts (AIGA) from 1988 to 1990. Bierut was elected to the Alliance Graphique Internationale, a global community of graphic designers, in 1989. In 2003, he was elected to the Art Directors Hall of Fame.

Bierut is a senior critic in Graphic Design at the Yale School of Art and writes frequently about design. He is a contributing editor to *ID* magazine and co-editor of the three-volume series *Looking Closer: Critical Writings on Graphic Design* published by Allworth Press. In 1998 he co-edited and designed the monograph *Tibor Kalman: Perverse Optimist*, published by Booth-Clibborn in 1998. He is also a founding contributor to the weblog designobserver.com.

Bierut's belief that for design to be successful it should be content driven and not necessarily focused on itself is clearly demonstrated by the breadth of his approach and diversity of client.

below
The centennial fundraising campaign for Princeton University, 1995, was organised around the theme 'With One Accord' and included event graphics and publications, all dedicated to engendering a sense of unity around the university's mission and goals. Bierut and his team at Pentagram designed *Re-thinking Design*, an annual publication for Mohawk Fine Papers, for eight years from 1992. Each issue explored a different theme of general interest to the design community, including the future of print, designing for subcultures, and vernacular design. A wide range of contributors participated in creating each issue.

above
Tibor Kalman: Perverse Optimist, was designed and co-edited by Bierut. Rather than reiterating the design tropes associated with M&Co's work, the monograph simply presents the material in a simple and respectful manner.

"Only by deliberating together about moral questions will we find mutual respect and common ground."

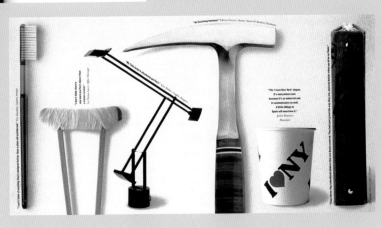

Bierut's clients range from multinationals to small cultural bodies but his solutions all testify to his belief in understanding the audience. The identity for the Minnesota Children's Museum, 1995, avoids the clichés of crayon scrawls and colourful shapes, using photographs of children's hands to emphasise the museum's 'hands-on' experience.

Many of Michael Bierut's comments endorse the central tenets of chapter 1. Graphic design is essentially about communication. The message generally originates with someone else. Designers have to decide if this is a message they want to support. 'Much, if not most, graphic design is about communicating messages, and many of those messages are intended to persuade,' he says. 'This places its practice clearly in the realm of politics, broadly defined, even when the message is not about "political" issues. About three years ago I decided not to participate in the design of messages that I didn't agree with. I never liked doing it, and no matter how much it paid, it was never enough.'

The introduction to this section discusses the absence of adequate definitions, that graphic designers seem confused as to their remit and the significance of their work. This has resulted loosely in two design camps, both defined by an attitude towards communication. Bierut brings clarity to this subject that almost renders it irrelevant. For him both are misguided. 'Some designers view themselves as passive receptacles and await clients who will fill their waiting vessels. Some designers view themselves as titanic fountainheads of self-expression, and view their clients as patrons who will derive satisfaction from helping them continue their personal growth. I think both positions are wrong, because they ignore so many other things: the audience, the content we work with, the outcome of the communication process.'

Bierut is a contributor to website www.designobserver.com, through which he recently explored this theme under the heading 'The World in Two Footnotes'. The footnotes he refers to were written by Nick Bell as addendums to his piece, 'The Steamroller of Branding', in the Autumn 2004 edition of *Eye* magazine. Bell defines the two design camps as 'agents of neutrality' and 'aesthetes of style'. He considers not only the differences but the similarities between the two. Bierut goes on to explore the notion of a 'third way', one which revisits former teachings, that design is a response to content. Bierut quotes Bell as advocating this solution: 'It's quite simple, it's been said before and so many times that it has become a cliché. And that is to design from the inside outwards.'

Bierut goes on to corroborate Bell's assertions. 'The practice of graphic design in general "must be inextricably tied to the content it is supposedly serving; make content the issue and resist making design the issue."'

As Bierut points out, this takes humility, an attribute often lacking 'in the ego-driven world of creative production'. The best design is not always the most groundbreaking or focused on itself. 'The excitement of the creative act was the reason I became a designer. But, as Mies van der Rohe said, I would rather be good than original.'

The World in Two Footnotes concludes: 'Designers are more often tempted to serve more urgently demanding gods: their clients on one hand, their inner muses on the other. What the world demands, however, is something more. Call it content, call it substance, call it meaning: it is the too-often-forgotten heart of what we do. It is the way out of the binary world that Nick Bell describes so well. It is the third choice. Choose content.'

In considering how communication works, chapter 1 shifts the focus away from the designer and towards the process. This encourages us to consider the message, the client, the audience and the designer's relationship to all three. Does Bierut see a designer's role as partly to visually educate client and audience? 'I get a little aggravated at the idea of designers "educating" anybody,' he replied. 'I feel that usually it is us designers who require the education. My assumption when I undertake an assignment is that I possess a unique but generalised expertise. My client, the specific message and the audience provide all the particulars that allow me to exercise my expertise effectively. My clients and audience may learn something about design, or "have their taste level raised", but that's only a by-product of an effective communications experience. Without the latter, the former is irrelevant.'

Bierut advocates a clear understanding of the audience as one element in a successful design process. Although 'this almost always requires a process of simplification, if not oversimplification... I think that creating categories is often an unavoidable by-product of the process. I find it much better to create bespoke categories that are relevant to the assignment at hand rather than to try to picture your audience squeezed into ready-made slots.'

When it comes to process theory and the technical level, Bierut's experience is similar to many designers. Early designer involvement generally yields the best results. 'The most interesting design projects are ones where you get involved early, helping to shape the message's substance as well as its form.' Bierut cites the work he and his team undertook to publicise a new building in New York by architect Renzo Piano as an example. 'Rather than the usual real estate brochure, we persuaded the owner to permit us to document the process of the building's creation, in all its messiness. To continue this "vérité" theme, the text for the piece was largely constructed from quotes from the architect and other principals in the project's development.'

Regarding effectiveness, Bierut is not against the idea of testing but points out that the process is flawed. 'My work is sometimes, but not always, subjected to this kind of testing. Sometimes it goes very well. In one instance, the client was so happy they sent me flowers. Other times you are stunned by the shallowness and inanity of the process. Somehow the right methodologies have not been created; perhaps they simply don't exist for many kinds of design.'

Chapter 1 considers the role of convention and cliché in graphic design work. Bierut acknowledges that 'human beings rely on both as a way to navigate through a confusing world,' but understands that 'designers tend to put a premium on innovation and invention'. The problem, of course, is that communication relies on some shared understanding and, as Bierut explains, this can only be challenged with some understanding and knowledge. 'An entirely new way to design, say, the table of contents in a magazine will not work unless it acknowledges the expectations that readers have about a table of contents. One doesn't necessarily have to enslave oneself to conventions, but you must understand why they exist, how they work, and consider how one might usefully deform, ignore, or overturn them.'

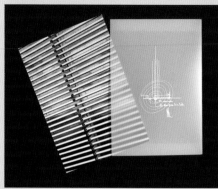

Does Bierut think that, essentially, modernism had got it right? 'Yes and no,' he replies. 'There is that great Phil Baines quote: "The Bauhaus mistook legibility for communication". Obviously, clarity is a good thing. But sterility and anonymity are bad things. The trick is to strike a balance between reason and rhetoric. To clarify, I'd like to use an analogy with clothing. The modernist ideal of "form follows function" would suggest that a clothing designer's primary responsibility is to provide warmth and comfort. Yet the way we dress sends all kinds of signals: social status, group affiliation, attitude about conventions, romantic availability. All of these are subtle, intuitive, emotional and contextual. Modernist ideology tends to undervalue the second, more "rhetorical" purpose of design.'

It seems Bierut could never completely ally himself with modernism. He doesn't want to categorise in order to understand or control and doesn't seem to feel any anxiety about the fluidity of the design process. He is happy to embrace Barthes's 'death of the author'. 'The designed object acquires a life of its own once it's out in the world. It no longer belongs to the designer or the client. The instability of the design process and its outcomes is what makes it fun for me. Unpredictability is interesting, not to mention instructive. It's what makes being a designer different from having an assembly line job.'

Although he writes about design and is extremely knowledgeable about the theory that underpins much of the practice, Bierut remains sceptical about how it is used. 'Because there is so little formal education in design theory, most successful designers seem to "make it up as they go along", and indeed this often means applying it to rationalise solutions after the fact, if at all.'

Bierut is happier to acknowledge that an understanding of design theory is one of many contributing elements in the production of 'good design'. 'Understanding design theory in general, as well as communications theory and social psychology, has been helpful to me in my work. However, I have found that knowing about a wide range of subjects – literature, history, politics, business – and being genuinely curious about the world has served me as well as any specific knowledge of design theory.'

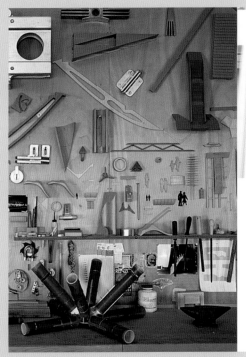

The New York Times' new headquarters by Renzo Piano is considered by some to be the most distinguished skyscraper in New York in over 50 years. In 2002 Pentagram produced a publication to promote the leasing of the space that the paper would not occupy. Bierut cites this as an example of a project that successfully utilised designers to shape the message's substance as well as its form. Bierut and his team took a journalistic approach, with text derived from published news accounts and images that document the design and building process from beginning to end, not just the slick renderings typical of leasing material.

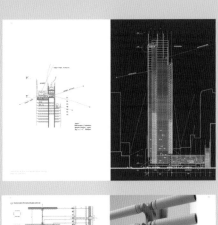

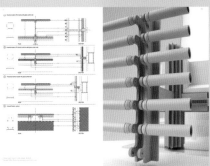

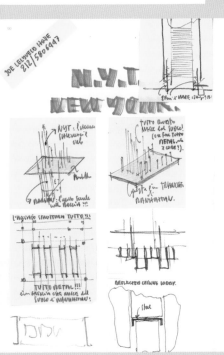

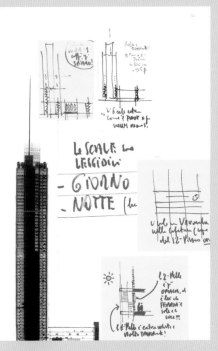

Communication

Introduction
Neville Brody
Michael Bierut

this and previous spread
Some of Bierut's work is seen and used by millions. He believes that its success is partly determined by an interest in understanding the client, the message they seek to convey and their audience.

Since 1995 Pentagram has worked as design consultants for United Airlines across all design disciplines, from graphics to interiors, product design to electronic communications, all with a goal to creating a simpler, more straightforward customer experience.

This extends to the naming and design of their low-cost airline, Ted; the name was derived from the last three letters of the parent's name, immediately signalling that this was literally a more casual and friendly 'part of United'.

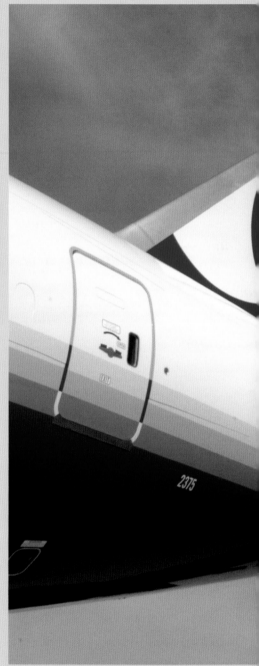

Visual Communication
Front matter
01 Communication
02 Culture
03 Conflict
End matter

01 **Questions in summary**

01 How does design theory relate to design practice?

02 Can designers ignore social and political factors when they work?

03 Who is central to the process of communication? The client, the audience, or the designer?

04 Is the view that design is an ideological practice a comfortable one?

05 What examples can you think of (or find) that illustrate the idea that meaning is arbitrary and that something that means one thing in one culture can mean something different in another?

06 Should designers consider how audiences will interpret their work before they put it into production? What problems come from ignoring feedback, or from ignoring your own judgement?

07 Does theory restrict creativity, or does it help it? Argue both sides. Return to this question when you have read the whole book.

ISBN-13: 978-2-940373-09-3
ISBN-10: 2-940373-09-4

9 782940 373093

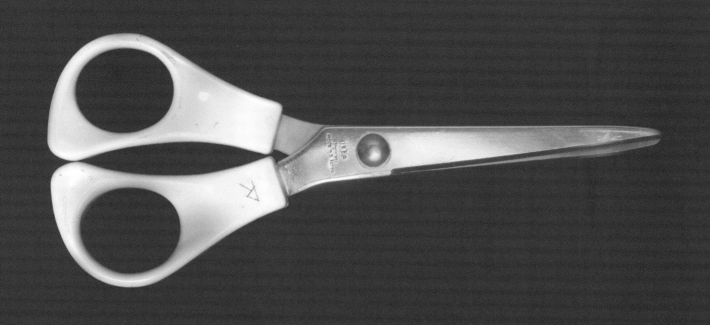

Odeon Leicester S

ODEON PRESENTS

STAR WARS EPI

SCREEN	ROW	SEAT
6	**F**	**21**

PRICE
£11.50

DATE
19/05/05

PROGRAMME TIME
8:15p

YOU WERE SERVED BY: A   AT: 6:08p
PRINTED ON: 25/03/05   AT TERMINAL: 98   TICKET SEQ: 00009516   PAID BY: Credit
ODEON CINEMAS LTD. VAT NUMBER: 572734N215

ODEON

01 Front Stalls

Visual Communication

Front matter
01 Communication
02 Culture
03 Conflict
End matter

02   # Culture

Aims of chapter 2

This chapter's theoretical essay introduces you to:

Definitions of 'culture' and 'popular culture' and the problems that arise from them. Is popular culture judged to be inferior because of its quantity, its quality or both?

Questions of meaning: is it invested in an item when it is created, or when it is used? Can designers really expect everyone to use their work in exactly the same way?

How advertising gives meaning to otherwise meaningless and identical objects through linking them to our basic human needs.

Theories about consumption as a means of acquiring status in an increasingly homogenous world. Is this something that is created by society itself, or by manufacturers of increasingly ephemeral products that become unfashionable as soon as they are purchased?

The concept of hegemony as a means by which social order is maintained by permitting low-level rebelliousness, before absorbing the products of that rebellion into wider society.

These key theories are then given real-life industry responses by three internationally famous designers:

Joan Farrer predicts a time when design will be based less around profit and desire and more around ecology and sustainability. Farrer is proud of her work for big retailers, but worries that the cheap availability of clothes is having an adverse effect on the environment as we buy things we do not need, only to discard them for new items.

Shin Azumi and Tomoko Azumi believe that it is possible to produce functional and beautiful design that lasts and is sold on the high street. For them originality is not about aesthetics, but is about ingenious and expedient use of materials and working cleverly within the constraints of any brief.

Culture

Introduction
What is culture?
All design is political: part two
Style and identity
Afterword

The Theory

Introduction

Everyday visual communication

Visual communication is not some dry theory or academic subject. Nor is it something that only the powerful or the elite engage in 'top down', as the end of chapter 1 may have suggested. It is an everyday lived practice, something we all engage in, consciously or otherwise.

Visit any shopping centre and you may come across a group of youths, each wearing similar styles and brands of clothes. What is both odd and fascinating about this is that the clothes are simultaneously being used as a sign of difference (setting the group apart from everyone else) and of belonging (a sign of membership of the group). We all do it: our clothes, our furniture, the films we see, the magazines we read, are a uniform, a marker of our belonging to a group, and simultaneously a signal of our difference from others.

How can something as simple as an item of clothing – and a mass-produced one at that – communicate something as powerful as a group dynamic and a sense of social isolation? This, it can be argued, is one of the main reasons for studying design – it is ill-considered to believe that design is all about 'the visual'. Even the most trivial piece of design has the potential to affect people's lives in some way. A designer who remains ignorant of this is undoubtedly ignoring the impact and importance of their practice.

In this chapter we look at definitions of 'culture' and of 'popular culture', and tie these in to views of what is worth preserving and studying about a society. But how does discussion of culture fit in with the concept of visual communication? Well, in the last chapter we looked at theories that initially considered communication as a transmission of a message from one party to another, and focused on the usual examples of government, industry and so on – 'dominant' groups communicating with the masses. This chapter looks at communication from the other side: how do the 'masses' articulate their own ideas to those in control, as well as to each other?

Although visual forms of communication are not the only way in which this happens, they are the most, well, 'visible'. And in the same way that we communicate in our spoken language without really thinking about the underlying grammar and syntax, we communicate visually using a commonly understood language. Just as we would not argue that writers are the only people who can produce words that mean something, this chapter should help you see that neither should we assume designers are the only people who can or do produce forms of visual communication.

But while it will become apparent that there are social drivers to everyday visual practices, there is a clear sense here that, at least, tastes for how we style our homes – the most personal of spaces – are being informed more and more by an army of 'professionals'. How the style gurus and fashion experts shape the design industry itself is a form of conflict we return to in the final chapter.

Keywords in this chapter

Mass culture
Cultural texts produced and consumed in large quantities and, according to some critics, intellectually undemanding and creatively limited.

Needs and desires
Things that are essential in order to survive or progress are 'needs'. Things that are not essential but we would like are 'desires'. For example, in order to write a letter we need a pen, but we might desire an expensive fountain pen. Turning our needs into desires, or creating desires without a need is often a purpose of visual communication.

Consumption
Buying and, importantly, using things. In particular, using things to produce meaning (e.g. wearing clothes to make a statement), is a key aspect of consumption here.

Conspicuous consumption
Buying or using something purely to show that you have good taste or the money to spend on things. Displaying designer labels on clothes or carrier bags from top stores might be an example.

Fashion cycle
The speed with which things move from being before their time to fashionable, to dated and eventually to being 'classic' and often fashionable once more.

Subculture
A culture within a larger culture that often has different beliefs or interests from the larger culture. Subcultures are commonly highly ritualised and participants are recognisable through their dress codes.

Counter-culture
Similar to a subculture but with a markedly more intellectual basis to their beliefs and a rational objection rather than a simple reaction.

Culture

Introduction
What is culture?
All design is political: part two
Style and identity
Afterword

What is culture?

27
For a fuller discussion of
the debates around the meaning
of 'popular culture' see
chapter 1 of *An Introduction
to Cultural Theory and Popular
Culture* by John Storey
(London: Prentice Hall, 1993).

'Culture' is a difficult word to define, and its meaning tends to shift depending on why you want to use it. Matthew Arnold defined it as 'the best that has been thought or said in the world', but this view tends to focus on what we might call 'high culture'.

The English cultural theorist Raymond Williams came up with three useful definitions of the term 'culture':

01
The process of a society's intellectual, spiritual and aesthetic development (e.g. the great philosophers, poets, artists etc.).

02
The particular way of life of a people, period or group (e.g. the development of literacy, the type of sports played, the celebration of festivals).

03
The works and practices of intellectual and especially artistic activity (e.g. poetry, novels, ballet, opera, fine art).

In other words, culture is often described in terms of people, events, practices and artefacts and, more often than not, it is 'the best' of these things that are considered to be worth preserving. Quite who decides what is culturally significant will be addressed again in chapter 3.

But in this chapter I want to focus on 'popular culture'[27]. What exactly is 'popular culture'? Well, if we keep in mind Williams's definitions of culture described on the left, our task is to understand the term 'popular'.

Tattoos are an ancient form of human decoration and can have a range of meanings – or none at all. But as this chapter shows, virtually everything we do, from the films we see to the clothes we wear and the furniture we buy, can be seen as a form of communication of our values and sense of identity.

British front windows traditionally were obscured by net curtains but are increasingly adopting a Dutch-like 'look inside our home' style. Notice the 'traditional' fake leading – many love the 'heritage' look and whether it is genuine or not is secondary to the illusory sense of nostalgia the look attempts to encapsulate.

01
Phenomenon evolving out of the consumerist and emerging youth culture of the 1950s and 1960s.

02
Its products are accessible and mass-produced work.

03
Work deliberately setting out to win favour with the masses or specific communities.

04
Culture produced by industry and consumed and popularised by word of mouth and the media.

Modern popular culture grew out of post-war consumerism and the rise of youth culture in America, which spread across the Western world. It manifested itself through music, writing, film, radio and television. Its production is related to industry, and its continuing success is derived from the way in which its products are received by the masses and 'fan' communities. The mechanisms of its production are not total; it works as a dialogue rather then being entirely imposed from above by the producers of meaning, who are simply quick to pick up on trends and feed them back in new forms to a captivated audience. Often, the signs and rituals of popular culture start in subcultures and become popularised by the mainstream. However, popular culture is generally perceived to be a cynical process for engaging the masses in a cycle of consumerist desire.

Popular culture is lived as well as preserved, and is composed not simply of the artefacts of everyday life, but of practices and rituals such as interaction and play. These things tend not to end up in museums, but without understanding how they were used their value and meaning might be consigned to history.

Culture

Introduction
What is culture?
All design is political: part two
Style and identity
Afterword

Critiques of mass culture

Films, books and music are increasingly similar and their creation and distribution are controlled by a few media organisations. If a film doesn't follow the formula, what chances does it have of being made or being shown?

To understand the modern phenomenon of twentieth century popular culture, it is worth paying some attention to earlier manifestations of popular culture, because its origins go further back – to the dawn of industrialisation.

The early part of the twentieth century saw an increased interest in the effects of industrialisation on society, and a perceived threat to centuries of practices and crafts that together formed the elusive identity of individual nations. In Britain, composers such as Vaughan Williams and Holst would travel the countryside collecting folk tunes that had been passed down from generation to generation. The same attempt to catalogue and preserve dying trades and practices went on in other fields too. 'Popular culture' here is what we might term folk or indigenous culture today, something innocent and 'authentic' that was under threat from modernity.

There was still a distinction between high and low culture, but the latter had a certain naivety that arguably was appreciated less for its anthropological value than for its distinctiveness – rough versus refined.

While for a few it was still possible to own beautifully crafted, unique artefacts, it became possible for the masses to have easy access to cheap, mass-produced copies of items enjoyed by the affluent. It became easier to buy reproductions and craftspeople began to struggle to produce their own artefacts. In short, society became driven less by a need to produce things for itself, and more by a desire to consume the products of a few large manufacturers. This in turn led to a perceived devaluation in the quality and artistic merit of those artefacts and a lack of authenticity.

Critics of this new trend towards mass culture focused on several areas. One was the perceived degradation in quality of items produced. Another was the predictable uniformity and facile nature of the artefacts, particularly in fiction, film and music. The Frankfurt School[28] saw the cultural industries as manipulative producers of an increasingly contrived homogenous mass culture. This can be seen quite clearly today in the endless reality TV show formats, soap operas that revolve around predictable plot lines, and derivative magazines that focus on celebrity gossip and allegedly 'real-life' stories. The readership consume them not because they are surprising or shocking, despite what the covers claim – but because they meet their expectations precisely and leave them wanting more. In a similar way to the folk tales and imagery of yesteryear, these magazines refigure and sensationalise the mundanity of everyday life for a public desperate for escapism, but to a place that is enduringly familiar. Films, television and pop music are open to similar criticism. We go to see films that have predictable plots and endings – even a 'twist' at the end is part of the pattern of expectation. Police dramas and living room-based sitcoms follow generic plot lines, and pop tunes are rhythmically and tonally similar – the moment these things start, we know how they are going to end.

28
The Frankfurt School was a group of neo-Marxist thinkers based in Frankfurt from 1930. It attempted to apply and adapt Marxist theory to the social conditions it was experiencing, rather than the ones that Marx experienced. Responsible for the development of what is known as 'critical theory', although the School's views on mass culture are criticised for being overly romantic, they are still a huge influence on new left thinking today. The School's analyses of aesthetics and mass culture are particularly relevant to visual communication, but their impact goes much further than that.

Theodore Adorno, a member of the Frankfurt School, described early consumers of such cultural products as 'victims' and the cultural industry as a dominant force that 'integrates its consumers from above'. Align this idea alongside the concept of audience categories discussed in chapter 1 and it becomes clear how and why this might work. Although the writer of a police drama may take great pride in the craft of its construction, the television company wants to deliver a familiar story to a target audience in order to increase viewing figures and therefore enhance its attractiveness to advertisers. Thus, the writer was probably commissioned to come up with something that ticks all the right boxes for a specified demographic. For the Frankfurt School, the political implications are clear: this process maintains public passivity towards institutions, but encourages active consumers of the goods. We are more likely to complain about the television schedules than the parliamentary timetable. In this sense, visual communication is an agent of ideology.

Even when the culture industry appears to be innovating and keeping consumers happy, critics identify a cycle of never-ending desire, fulfilment and eventual disillusionment (Figure 5). The effect is to keep the masses preoccupied with things that don't matter, and to quell any desire for political and social change.

The people being satisfied are not the consumers (who if anything find satisfaction frustratingly beyond their reach), but manufacturers, their shareholders, the media (who depend on advertisers for their revenue) and the government. This process can be seen most clearly in the way advertising works.

Figure 5
Consumption depends upon satisfying a demand created by the producer, but it is never fulfilled and always deferred – so the cycle begins again.

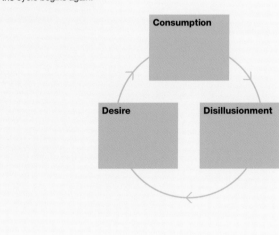

Culture

Introduction
What is culture?
All design is political: part two
Style and identity
Afterword

Designing desire – how advertisers use signs

Human needs and desires

29
Decoding Advertisements: Ideology and Meaning in Advertising by Judith Williamson (London: Marion Boyars, 1978).

In chapter 1 we explored how objects and symbols come to have meaning. But many of the things we take for granted in life have no real meaning beyond their function. A car is a car, at the end of the day, and shampoo is basically the same no matter who makes it. Judith Williamson, in her book *Decoding Advertisements*[29] points out that the products that get advertised the most are those that are fundamentally the same. The purpose of the ad is to differentiate similar products from one another. They do this by creating characteristics they don't really possess and emphasising the way in which the product is new, improved and current. Their meanings are appropriated from the world we live in – a world in which we all have a set of basic needs. Psychologists claim that when our basic needs are met we feel balanced, but when they are not we are driven to restore the balance. Our primary needs are related to survival, while our secondary needs are related to our family, peer group and society in general. Abraham Maslow devised a hierarchy of human needs (see Figure 6, below), a pyramid-like structure in which we strive to move from our base needs to higher levels of self-determination and independence.

We need to satisfy one level before we can move up to the next. Until we have satisfied our basic needs, levels beyond this represent desires, things we want but don't need. This motivates us and we are aroused by anything that offers us a route to the peak of our desires.

We don't need an expensive new car or designer shampoo. But we do need to feel safe, loved, and that we can realise our potential. This is how advertising does its job. It sets up an imbalance by offering us things we don't need in return for things we do. And so a car comes to mean safety and security, as well as signalling status to others; shampoo is linked to sexual attraction and gratification; baked beans signal family security and contentment; the latest clothes promise a new, more exciting lifestyle and individuality, while also reassuring us that we belong.

Figure 6
Maslow's hierarchy of human needs. Our ultimate goal (to achieve our potential) can only be satisfied if everything else is in place first.

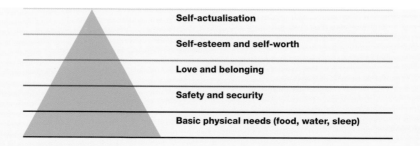

Self-actualisation

Self-esteem and self-worth

Love and belonging

Safety and security

Basic physical needs (food, water, sleep)

There are a few products that can't be shown in advertisements – toilet paper, sanitary towels, dentures. So these items have long been advertised by attaching them to something marginally related, but which pinpoints some desirable characteristic – the 'Andrex' puppy is one well-known example. The relative 'softness' of its toilet paper is compared to that of other manufacturers. The 'Charmin' brand uses similarly friendly motifs for its advertising. More recently the makers of the 'Velvet' brand has shown a series of ads depicting people's behinds with the slogan 'Love your bum', which borrows the same gentle approach to a difficult product, but using more direct language.

Humour and puzzles are another way of raising the desirability of a brand because we can share in them or feel superior about solving them. In Europe, the Skoda brand is well respected, but in the UK it has long been a metaphor for eccentric design and unsophisticated production.

When the brand was re-launched in the UK, the manufacturer played to its former image and made fun of the preconceptions. A direct mail campaign, for example, sent badges to tie in with an ad in which characters commiserated with people whose cars had been 'vandalised' by having one stuck on their car (which was, of course, a Skoda, but didn't meet the expectations). The brochure, left, makes a simple statement about common sense, and attempts to rewrite popular opinion by casting the reader as a clever and forward-thinking consumer.

Culture

Introduction
What is culture?
All design is political: part two
Style and identity
Afterword

Mass culture and meaning

52 53

Objects such as furniture have no essential 'meaning' beyond their function. Something important is missing from this picture...

But this critique of the culture industry may be misdirecting the emphasis. It is easy to dismiss mass culture as being intrinsically banal, and despair of blind consumerism.

However, it might be said that when a more sophisticated consumer attends an 'art' film, or purchases a piece of designer furniture or clothing, the level of its exposure and meaning is limited in comparison to a mass-produced item. Instead, the focus of consumption is on the status of the designer or director. In addition, the number of people who can afford to buy the brand is limited by the cost, hence perpetuating the sign of exclusivity. When people go to see a mainsteam film or buy an off-the-peg dress, the value is greater because of the sheer numbers of its circulation. The novel *A Clockwork Orange*[30] is regarded as an example of classic literature because it has something profound to say about the human condition, but its 'literariness' makes it less accessible and therefore 'meaningful' than a mainstream title such as *Bridget Jones's Diary*[31], which has been read by more people and which also discusses aspects of the human condition, albeit in a more accessible way[32].

Thus, which is more valuble? The authenticity of the designer dress, the art film or the literary work, or the artefacts of popular culture? Perhaps it is unfair to compare. The true meaning of an artefact only becomes apparent when it is consumed. The same film has different meanings when we watch it alone, in the cinema with friends or at home with family. A sofa stops being a piece of design and becomes a place where you feel comfortable or where you can invite friends. A piece of music has different meanings if it is played while you dance, perform housework, or for relaxation. A dress has different meanings if you feel good when you are wearing it, if it attracts attention or if somebody else turns up wearing the same thing.

Meaning is not simply invested in something at the site of its creation, but when it is recreated at the site of consumption. This, in a sense, is what is often meant by the term 'popular culture', it is culture we create from the artefacts that are created for us.

30
Anthony Burgess's novel *A Clockwork Orange* (1962) is notable for its use of a made-up language, 'Nadsat', which makes the book difficult to read without some perseverance. The central character, Alex, is seemingly beyond redemption but then brainwashed into being a model citizen. The moral dilemma becomes one of choice: Alex becomes a law-abiding citizen, but has no choice in the matter. The novel was turned into a film by Stanley Kubrick and was famously banned in the UK for its depictions of violence, becoming an instant cult classic.

31
Bridget Jones's Diary (1996) by Helen Fielding, tells the story of heroine Bridget and her obsession with her weight, her job and her love life. It is told in the style of a diary using simple language and abbreviations, and was turned into a highly successful film in 2001, with a sequel (based on 1999's follow-up *The Edge of Reason*) released in 2004.

32
The contrast I have used here is intended to be provocative. Bridget Jones's struggles are more relevant to many today, particularly to women in their thirties (a key target market) than Alex's, and the everyday language and form of the novel aided its success. This success might also consign it to near the bottom of a list of 'great' novels, while *A Clockwork Orange*, which is less accessible and more intellectually challenging, is widely considered to be closer to the top. The distinction here is between what is 'great' and what is 'popular', which are two kinds of value producing two kinds of meaning, neither of which may be superior to the other.

The humble sofa has become something of a style icon, but it isn't just for sitting on. An old sofa has been the location for some of our best and worst moments in life. That's why people buy them – not just to sit on. Interestingly, second-hand sofas decrease in financial value, but increase in use and symbolic value.

The socialisation of consumption

To subscribe to this concept, the idea that the consumer is waiting to be manipulated, is to misunderstand the theory. No-one consumes the products of culture in a vacuum – cultural consumption is profoundly socialised and therefore our choices and tastes are shaped by our social relationships and environment. Second, no-one encounters cultural products one at a time, we receive them accumulatively, are bombarded with competing messages, and each one is shaped by the body of messages already received. It is true, as the Frankfurt School suggests, that these competing products and messages are largely formulaic, identical, but the circumstances and the order in which they are consumed are not. Let's look again at magazines. While the subject matter may not vary much from edition to edition, readers use the content in an interactive way: as a source of entertainment and, importantly, for the purpose of social inclusion and engagement.

There is a glimmer of hope here, an escape from the doom-laden view of ideology defined in chapter 1 and the views of the Frankfurt School. To see it we need to think less of consumption as 'purchase' and more about consumption as 'communication'.

Two more definitions of 'popular culture'

At this point it is useful to introduce two new definitions of popular culture:

05
A postmodernist view: no distinction between high and low.

06
Culture resulting from resistance to the dominant culture.

The first view, the idea that there is no distinction between 'high' and 'low' culture, is a common one – but, arguably, mostly among the 'educated' who have easy access to a range of cultural traditions and artefacts. If you are a university undergraduate or graduate you may encounter diverse cultures, in the form of classical music, theatre and literature at the same time as dance music, club cultures and sounds, tastes and concepts from other countries and ethnic groups. This 'fusion' of cultures is a feature of our 'postmodern' society, but we must be careful not to assume that just because an informed middle class experiences such diversity, that everyone else does. On closer inspection, cultural fusion may be less pervasive than it first appears.

It is the final definition of 'popular culture' – as a form of resistance to the dominant culture – which informs the rest of this chapter. It isn't about making quantitative or qualitative differences between different cultural practices or artefacts, but differences in meaning. In this view, the celebration of Christmas, the wearing of certain clothes, the decoration of our homes, and so on, and the messages and meanings these communicate, can be viewed politically.

Culture

Introduction
What is culture?
All design is political: part two
Style and identity
Afterword

All design is political: part two

Hegemony

The concept of ideology as outlined in chapter 1 identifies its pervasive power, but also that it is not total. It posits that while ordinary people are the target of a cynical cycle of consumerism and desire, waiting to be informed about the latest new trend, it also suggests that production is flexible, that sometimes culture can be produced from below, or that cultural artefacts are used in ways that producers may not have anticipated.

To look at this relationship more closely, we need a better model, one that allows for the variety of ways in which we respond to the diverse range of messages we receive from institutions such as the government and the various forms of the media, as well as those from our friends, family and complete strangers, and the messages we generate ourselves.

33
'Hegemony' was conceptualised by Italian Marxist Antonio Gramsci in the 1930s. Most definitions of hegemony focus on its political aspects. For a good explanation of its cultural implications see John Hartley's definition in *Key Concepts in Communication and Cultural Studies* by Tim O'Sullivan, et al. (London: Routledge, 1994) pp 133–135.

34
One of the objections often heard in relation to some of the theories covered in this book is that a lot of them are 'common sense'. But the problem with common sense is that it's only obvious when it's pointed out.

Think about it. Society is rarely controlled via domination and coercion. If we are forcibly told to do something against our will, eventually we rebel. However, many more times we are 'persuaded' to do things we wouldn't normally do voluntarily. In other words, we consent to behave in a way that primarily suits the interests of others through some form of negotiation. In fact, this is a common method of control and starts at a young age when we are asked to do something (tidy your room, for example) in return for some form of parental reward. The parental model of negotiation simply becomes replaced by other forms of negotiation with authority figures when we grow up. At the end of the day, we still behave the way producers of culture and institutions demand, but we feel we have at least got something in exchange – the power dynamic remains stable and unchallenged.

This process of negotiation or exchange is known as hegemony[33]. It helps to explain how, throughout history, some influential groups or classes have managed to predominate over another group or class without resorting to totalitarianism – and how those groups who do impose rule often end up losing it suddenly and violently.

A society that allows a reasonable amount of protest is, according to the theory of hegemony, less likely to change suddenly. It's in societies that forbid protest that sudden and violent change takes place. Democracy could be argued to be rather less free than we think as it prolongs a single world view.

Hegemony says that as long as we think we have our say, we'll accept the common sense view. If the majority agree about something, does that make it right? In a hegemonic society, this might not mean that everyone is happy with the outcome, but it does ensure that there is space for negotiation and resistance.

In its most basic terms, a hegemonic culture is one in which our co-operation is guaranteed through a process of negotiation. It maintains a hierarchy, contains imbalances, but is broadly consensual. It works only insofar as the various groups feel that their needs are heard and met. We remain agents of autonomy within broadly accepted social and cultural parameters – and those parameters are elastic, depending on the economic and political climate. In this way it is a constantly shifting, organic form, that, while far from perfect, mostly works.

In a hegemonic culture, we may not always be happy, but we have some sort of personal and collective power, whether it is at the ballot box, using the TV remote control, not buying a particular product, or even abstaining from decision-making processes altogether.

Hegemony doesn't escape ideology. It is still an ideological process, but is more subtle and co-operative than the description of ideology suggested in chapter 1. Ideology, in hegemonic terms, becomes natural, fluid, invisible, or 'common sense', if you like[34]. This is evident in the use of phrases like 'people are saying' or 'there was widespread outrage' in news reports or the speech of politicians, or the use of the inclusive 'we' or 'let's'. For example, 'let's take a look at the main stories tonight' is a common phrase on news programmes, which sets up a cosy familiarity with the viewer as both individual and part of the collective community.

In cultural studies, visual communications are a major focus for analyses of hegemony, concentrating on how the images and objects produced by and for us help us to make sense of ourselves and the world around us; and how in turn this sense fits in with the needs of the institutions (such as the state, the law, industry, media, families, universities). It helps to answer why, among other things, we buy things we don't need, or why fashion and tastes change.

There is no conspiracy here; institutions are not working together to keep 'us' in order. But an understanding of a hegemonic society helps to explain how, over time, the needs of these 'cultural agencies' come to be accepted and embedded. It also explains how hegemony can never be total; within it are counter-hegemonic processes that resist the world view of the dominant groups. As we shall see, this can have important cultural implications.

Protests against the invasion of Iraq in 2004 often took a humorous approach. Humour is often used as a powerful and subversive tool for protest – and is much less dangerous than other forms of confrontation. With hegemony, it might be argued that smaller forms of protest ultimately reinforce the world view they critique, because how can a society that allows 'free speech' be bad?

Culture

Introduction
What is culture?
All design is political: part two
Style and identity
Afterword

Cultural consumption – as visual communication

Conspicuous consumption – buying to communicate

In pre-industrial Western societies, one of the only ways for the affluent, powerful classes to display status was to build vast estates and engage in 'conspicuous leisure' – making sure that they were seen to not be doing any work, while their tenants visibly supported their lifestyle.

As modern Western society moved from pre-industrial to industrial, the relatively discrete presence of the ruling classes meant that leisure was much less impressive as a means of communicating status. In an imperialist age, something more tangible was required. Instead, those in positions of power and wealth began to employ various means to make public displays of their status. Clothes and jewellery became an impressive means to set themselves apart from the masses. Being 'smart', was a clear indicator that you were not employed to do any form of labour, but might perform some kind of work. Being ostentatious was a sign that you did not do any kind of work at all. Other signs of status included modes of transport, travel, entertainments and making or contributing to charitable and worthy works, such as building chapels, hospitals and homes for workers. Of course, demonstrations of charity cannot be ascribed solely to the desire to 'show off' status; many landowners felt a sense of responsibility towards those less fortunate than themselves. This was part and parcel of the patriarchal class system – and it was in their own best interest to be benevolent. And, clearly, with that responsibility came the prestige and respect afforded to those who invested in their status in such a profound way.

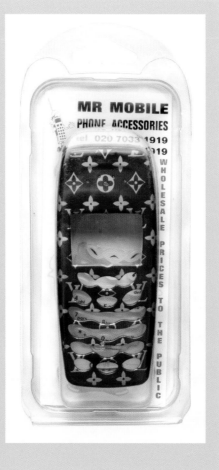

The vogue for customisation reached its peak with changeable mobile phone covers, screensavers, wallpaper and ringtones. The phone is no longer about communicating with the person on the other end of the line, but with anyone within view or earshot.

Fashion and urban living

In 1903, German sociologist Georg Simmel observed the way clothes became a way of expressing identity rather than status. He noticed that people living in the rapidly expanding city of Berlin found it difficult to adapt to the anonymity urban living brought with it. Those who could afford to used clothes as a means of expressing and maintaining their sense of individuality and identity.

This use of fashion as a sign system is often described as 'social practice', something we actively (though often subconsciously) engage in. One group seeks to imitate the other, which in turn drives those seeking to differentiate themselves to devise new forms of expression. These soon become imitated and the cycle begins again.

At the time he was writing, Simmel described fashion as 'a product of class distinction'. Today, this is much less the case, but nevertheless the kinds of clothes we choose and wear are an indicator of status. While clothes can mark out different groups – members of sub-cultures, for example – essentially, fashion operates as a system of signage within as well as between different social classes.

Simmel's views appear somewhat dated today, but they are still useful. It is important to understand how consumption reflects cultural values, and, to do so, we need to borrow from semiotics to view consumption as a language in which the things we buy are signs of where and how we fit into the fabric of society.

There's a wide choice of weekly and monthly magazines available. Do these publications reflect the way we live – or do they shape it?

Culture

Introduction
What is culture?
All design is political: part two
Style and identity
Afterword

Hardly the uniform predicted by futurologists, the clothes we wear are increasingly diverse, yet no one really stands out. We can be individual, with confidence. So why do we feel the need to follow fashion?

Style and democracy

We live in a mass-produced world. We have to look long and hard to find clothes, food and furniture that are not reproduced by the thousands, or even millions. Those who are positioned outside of the mass market tend to be those who possess the cultural capital – the knowledge, inside information, transport, and money – to buy into what might be perceived to be the 'authentic' world. The rest of us tend to buy into imitations of the major trends, to emulate the originals.

Popular films and books that attempted to portray life in the year 2000 imagined a future where everybody dressed and lived identically. Mass production, whether seen as an effect of totalitarianism or utopia, was seen as a homogenising force. Yet look around us and we see – what? Despite the fact that we mostly buy our clothes and furnish our homes from the same few retailers, and are as likely to own the same brands not just as our neighbours but also as people on the other side of the world, we look far from identical. In fact, we all appear to dress completely individually. Certainly there are common looks and styles, but within those groups there is a definite sense of difference and choice.

Mass culture and its consumption can be seen not as a wholly homogenising force, but one which involves a large degree of differentiation. We are driven not by a search for happiness per se, but by a search for the ability to realise our values and desired way of life. While critics of mass culture see it as a product of our capitalist society, we could equally see our economic system as a result of our collective desire for social identity, difference and belonging (something I come back to in chapter 3).

In this scenario, designers are what theorist Pierre Bourdieu calls 'cultural intermediaries': people who interpret and mediate the aspirations of society and produce cultural artefacts to satisfy it. It is important to remember, of course, that designers do not exist outside of culture, but actively participate in it as consumers as well. In fact, in this way, they are in a unique position as both producer and consumer of culture.

Style and identity

The home front

Through the keyhole

Even before it became feasible for ordinary people to own their own homes, the domestic space was regarded as the one where privacy was reasonably assured. But there is another aspect of the living space that makes a home: style. In our public life our capacity for visual expression and communication is severely limited. There are formal and informal codes that regulate what we wear, how we style our hair, and so on. Shop workers and those employed in service industries wear uniforms that require them to conform. Office workers are expected to dress smartly (men are arguably more constrained here), while those working with food have to wear hats and overalls and remove jewellery.

But home is where we can express our personalities. The codes at home are our own; we are no longer under public scrutiny or any form of expectation to conform.

When we operate in the wider world we often conform to the expectations of others, in the type of house we live in, the suit we wear, the car we drive. When we get home we can become ourselves once again. Or at least, that used to be true.

Are our homes becoming more public? Do we make them look like the magazines so we can feel happy in ourselves, or so we can invite people round to gaze at our good taste and success?

Private versus public

Critics of modern life blame the increased sense of isolation of modern living on high-rise blocks of flats, conversions of houses into units, and the growth in the number of single-occupant households. In some cases it is rare to meet our neighbour and rarer still to have them round to our homes. It isn't even the kind of buildings we live in or the arrangement of living spaces per se that are the source of the problem, but that our social relationships have evolved from the closeknit communities of yesteryear into differently organised kinds of communities.

Far from being less sociable, we are simply socialising away from home a great deal more than was once the case. We eat out quite regularly, visit the cinema more than in recent times and meet friends in cafés, pubs and bars throughout the week. We are also communicating with one another in more virtual ways than ever before. Forming new relationships no longer depends on geography. We can meet over the phone or the Web. Society is changing, and while it is easy to suggest we are becoming more isolated, there is plenty of evidence to tell us we are living our lives increasingly publicly.

If this is the case, one might imagine the home would become a haven from the world, styled around the needs of its occupants. But this is not the case. Whereas our homes have always reflected the styles and taste of the times, we have never been so self-conscious about the look of our homes as we are today. Visiting different houses today is akin to walking into the pages of a catalogue or a furniture showroom. Everything looks neat and consciously 'stylish'. It is as though the home has become yet another public sphere, kept permanently tidy just in case visitors (or photographers) arrive unexpectedly. The home appears to have become another reflection of a dominant ideology about how we should live. What is going on?

Our expectations of what our home, and the homes of our friends, should look like are increasingly dictated by the editors of magazines and their advertisers. We judge and feel judged on the state of our increasingly visible lifestyle.

Real homes have piles of
washing up in the sink,
old newspapers on the floor,
stains on the coffee table
and damp towels in the
bathroom. Well, it's a look.

Culture

Introduction
What is culture?
All design is political: part two
Style and identity
Afterword

Nosy neighbours

35
Part of the reason why so many of us are addicted to these house makeover programmes is because the transformation is instananeous and complete. So rarely are we able to transform our homes in this way in real life. The programmes enable us to fantasise about duplicating the effects on our own homes, but the watching itself satisfies the desire.

36
It's worth pointing out that even in the world of haute couture fashion, commercial pressures play a part. Retailers and fabric companies will often advise designers on colours and cloths for coming seasons.

37
A feminist approach to this issue would produce a different, and valid, viewpoint; readers are advised to explore research into the way the fashion industry has shaped, rather than reflected, the lifestyles and roles of women.

Home make-over programmes now dominate the schedules, from daytime TV to prime time and beyond. Whole channels are dedicated to the subject of moving, renovating or restyling the home.

The formats of some of these programmes, particularly the BBC's *Changing Rooms*, have been translated successfully for other countries, reflecting an international obsession with home styling. Magazine titles have proliferated and sales increased in line with this trend. Most make heavy use of 'the expert' pitted against the comically naive crimes-against-style of ordinary people. We are invited to laugh somewhat smugly at these people, while no doubt making mental notes about our own inept home decoration.

Within minutes the residents are cleared out, and we are treated to long panning shots, complete with voiceover telling us where these people are going wrong. Later, the shots will cut from 'before' to magical 'after' as we see the fruits of the experts' labours[35]. Everything is pristine. Plump cushions sit at angles of posed casualness on spotless sofas. Aside from the half-filled cafetière and carefully arranged biscuits, there is no evidence anyone lives here. The bathroom is clean and sparkling. Seashells and pebbles are decoratively arranged on dust-free shelves and clean towels hang on polished rails. And on the farmhouse dining table cereal bowls are arranged on dinner plates, a rosy red apple placed in each one.

Something is not quite right here. What does the coffee table look like stained not by varnish, but by a few months of accidentally spilled wine? Where are the magazines on the floor and the permanent indentations on the sofa cushion? Where are the pet hairs and scratched surfaces? Where are the damp towels in the bathroom and the soap scum around the taps? Where are the clothes on the bedroom floor and the crumbs on the kitchen worktop? Where are the people? These houses are unreal.

But the show homes we witness on TV reflect an enormous change in the way we live our private lives. We have always consulted experts on how to transform our homes, but the desire appears to be more pervasive than ever. Our parents and grandparents are fond of telling us that their generation bought things to last, but today, rather than genuinely loved and worn furniture, we crave the pristine faux distressed look and sterile cleanliness of the photo-shoot. Why do we want to live as though we are on TV? Who are we seeking to please? The home has become a vehicle for one of the most conspicuous forms of visual communication. The phrase 'An Englishman's home is his castle' is an enduring one. We are still impressed by status and want our homes to reflect that and we are willing to buy into current trends to do it. The only difference now is that most of us can afford to do that because the look is easier to create than ever before.

The wardrobe

What is 'fashion'?

Fashion is not the preserve of the experts. Increasingly, we buy our clothes from a wide range of outlets and can pick up an entire outfit for a dinner party in the same shop as we buy the ingredients for the meal we intend to serve.

We've already looked at fashion as a form of social catch-up, but 'fashion' is an odd word, particularly when applied to clothes. For some, the term means the latest designs previewed on the catwalks of Paris and Milan, worn by the rich and famous. But for most, fashion means the clothes being worn by a group of people at a particular time. The two terms appear to be mutually exclusive. For the purposes of this discussion we are concerned mainly with 'popular' fashion rather than 'high' fashion. The biggest clothes retailers are supermarkets such as Asda and Tesco in the UK and Wal-Mart in the USA – not the specialist boutiques and chain stores – and their dominance of the market is growing. Although many fashion students dream of one day working for the big fashion labels or running their own, it is on the high street that fashion operates in a meaningful and communicative way.

With high fashion, designers determine the styles that are being worn[36], and the models and actresses who wear them very publicly are essentially billboards for the designer's 'vision'. But on the high street, while the collections are basically imitations of high fashion, there is a democratic aspect; spotting trends months before they happen means keeping an eye on the many different influences that shape tastes. In the early twentieth century, the discovery of Tutankhamen's tomb led to a fashion for all things Egyptian; during times of war tastes can reflect the turmoil of the times. After 9/11 one commentator predicted that fashion would return to the Hippy styles of cotton shirts, wide skirts, and long hair – and it did – but it also saw the influence of military styles, popularised by Madonna's somewhat ironic and confrontational look of the moment.

Designers do not dictate style alone. The relationship between designer and consumer is mediated by buyers for the big stores and, as with any form of communication, the potential exists for getting it wrong, as has happened most recently and publicly with the fall from grace of Marks & Spencer in the UK, once a byword for value on the high street.

The point is that the fashion industry offers designers an example of how style is not simply the creation of 'experts', but is a negotiation between the designer, retailer, media and the consumer. Fashion allows people to express their identity, to transform themselves, or to simply adopt what they think is the acceptable look, using the latest magazines as guides. But it is also a social experience, particularly, though not exclusively, for women[37].

Culture

Introduction
What is culture?
All design is political: part two
Style and identity
Afterword

The fashion cycle

How does fashion work, in the sense that something may be 'fashionable' or 'unfashionable'? Why, for example, did flared trousers go from super-stylish in the 1970s to inspire protests of 'I can't believe we used to wear things like that' in the 1980s and 1990s to being 'in' again? Why is it that the moment a fashion becomes widely accepted and worn it suddenly becomes unfashionable? Why do some people look out of date, but before long they're fashion icons?

We looked at some of the factors affecting the adoption of fashion earlier in this chapter. According to Laver's Law (which is more tongue in cheek than a hard-and-fast rule), costume goes through a 160-year life cycle.

Indecent	10 years ahead of its time
Shameless	5 years ahead of its time
Smart	Now
Dowdy	1 year after its time
Hideous	10 years after its time
Amusing	20 years after its time
Quaint	50 years after its time
Charming	70 years after its time
Romantic	100 years after its time
Beautiful	150 years after its time

38
This is no coincidence – why do all the different stores seem to agree on what clothes should look like months in advance?

Attitudes towards items of fashion change with time. The mini skirt of the 1960s was a radical response to the long skirts of the 1950s, but in the 1970s the mid-length and long skirt became vogue again. Fashion is cyclical. It makes use of the past to reinvent itself, a bricolage of eras and influences, and always controversial.

While the generalisation is intriguing, fashions don't follow the same pattern – some styles last a few weeks, others are around for years. And some survive through different variations; jeans, for example, have gone through several shades of blue, black and bright colours, faded, torn, too long, low-slung and tight enough to restrict circulation.

However, the pace of fashion's cycle has quickened dramatically since the start of the century, and more so in the past few decades. This has a great deal to do with the appearance of couturiers in mid-nineteenth century Paris who dealt exclusively with the upper-middle classes, and for whom it was good business sense to devise new fashions every decade or so. Today, the decade-long cycle has increased to being a seasonal one – if not shorter. We have several factors to thank for this: cheaper clothes, a more competitive market, increased affluence among consumers, less marked class divisions, and the influence of the media. It is the latter contribution that leads to a great deal of criticism of fashion as a form of ideology, designed to perpetuate the life of the fashion producers to make profits and grow financially.

Simmel's model of fashion, discussed earlier, may have been accurate in the nineteenth and early twentieth centuries, but it misses important aspects of the way fashion works today. There are, broadly, three sources of 'fashion' today: the haute couture designers who are well-known, but fairly exclusive; manufacturers and high-street buyers who filter and adapt the catwalk designs for mass production and consumption; and the fashion produced every day by ordinary people. By this I mean the fashion that is appropriated and refigured by each of us to reflect our own identities. Very few people look like they have been dressed to replicate the outfits seen in catalogues and shop windows. We rarely wear entire outfits bought from the same shop; instead, we select our wardrobe from an array of sources, piecing together our own personal style. It is DIY design or, to give it its proper name, 'bricolage' (which is French for 'do it yourself'). Academics and commentators of the sociological aspects of visual culture often celebrate this form of visual communication. Bricolage is a form of cultural hegemony that allows people to express their individuality from the materials provided to them by the producers of culture, and is prevalent in studies of subcultures, which we will discuss on the following pages.

Critics point to flaws in this last category of fashion devotees. Firstly, the fashions from which this group buy their clothes have already been filtered and sold to us by the fashion buyers. And even though individual stores claim their own 'look', it is evident that every season they all seem to make much the same choices about which colours, cuts and fabrics are fashionable for that season[38]. In this way, a bricolage approach to dress is only provisionally subversive. It works with predetermined styles which are simply worn in a new way. This category is still contained within and defined by the dominant modes of fashion.

Despite the apparent uniformity of the apparently endless choice available to us (a 'choice-less choice'),it still allows us to express our individuality by offering a choice at all, while simultaneously minimising the chance that we stand out too much from everyone else. Compared with no choice at all and complete uniformity at one end of the spectrum, or so much choice we risk standing out too much and inviting the derision of the fashionistas, the middle ground of moderate fashion risk-taking may be preferable. Being individual, while at the same time fitting in, are, as we saw in Maslow's hierarchy of human need, two of our highest aspirations. It is visual communication's equivalent of a stage whisper – it communicates something, but not too loudly.

But what if we want to shout? What if we want to be different and resist the dominant trends of what we should look like and how we should behave? What if we have fundamental problems with the producers of all aspects of our culture: politics, the media, the fashion industry? What if we simply want to rebel? Next we look at the subcultures.

Culture

Introduction
What is culture?
All design is political: part two
Style and identity
Afterword

Subcultures and counter-cultures

The term 'subculture' refers to any minority group with a shared set of beliefs, values or lifestyle that resists the dominant culture. While subcultures are popularly understood to be a phenomenon of 'youth', they can also reflect ethnic, religious or sexual groups of any age.

One of the distinguishing features of a subculture is that it tends to have a less visibly intellectual basis – unlike a 'counter-culture', which is motivated by a guiding philosophy. It is a spontaneous reaction to something in the dominant culture and expresses itself by appropriating and reinterpreting the symbols of that culture. Consequently, studies of subcultures have focused on the significance of style as a means of expression and identity, including clothes, but also music and language. Other components of subculture include a respect for an internal group hierarchy, and the use of rituals, from simple gatherings to forms of dance. Because of the importance of style in the evolution of subcultures, studies have drawn on semiotics to decode symbols used. This can only be partially successful.

Some of the most important twentieth-century subcultures include the Mods, Rockers, Teddy Boys, Skinheads and Punks, each of which displayed classic identifying factors. In 1980s Britain, the Skinheads were characterised by their shaven heads, jeans, t-shirts, braces and Doc Marten shoes, and considered to be symbols of an increasingly disenchanted and disenfranchised, largely male population, protesting against a fast-disappearing industrial age. It was a deliberate revolt against the values of a growing middle class and conservative culture, from which the Skinheads were isolated by lack of cultural and political capital. By adopting their look and attitude, a member was attempting to take charge and to define himself rather than be passively defined by a dominant culture.

For a subculture such as the Skinheads – and perhaps the Mods that preceded them – dress and ritual became a means through which to 'negotiate' their position on the periphery of society and the dominant culture.

Counter-cultures (the Hippies, above), as opposed to subcultures (the Teddy Boys, above far right), resist the status quo but from an intellectual standpoint. For this reason they are perceived to be a greater threat to the dominant culture.

Subcultures are a form of hegemonic resistance that is negotiated, sometimes initially quite violently, but ultimately absorbed into the mainstream. By provoking a reaction subcultures bolster the system they oppose as their gradual navigation from the periphery to the centre supports an inclusive society.

Mods are another example. Like Skinheads, Mods were largely working class, but tended to be employed in low- to mid-grade jobs. They responded to the dominant culture of the 1960s (which promoted consumption in the post-war economic boom, combined with a strong work ethic) by dressing in a specific brand of 'smart' clothes, different from the underdressing of the Skinheads, but which still set them apart. They spent what money they had on luxuries such as clothes, alcohol, drugs and mopeds. For Mods, the rebellion was about the contradiction between the authoritarianism of an outdated post-war culture and their desire to be liberated by a new youth-orientated era.

Any analysis of subcultures is necessarily problematic. One must consider the specifics. First, they tend to be selective and focus on white male working-class culture, ignoring the role of women, for example. They also tend to be overly romanticised, centring on class-based struggle and therefore largely subjective. The third problem, hinted at earlier, is that in analysing the meaning of signs, such as the Punk's safety pin jewellery – an example of 'bricolage', in which an item from the dominant culture is imbued with new meaning for the subculture – the spontaneous aspect of subcultures might become lost in the very articulation of their signs. For example, a group of people do not simply decide one day to start wearing Doc Martens as an ironic statement about the loss of traditional industrial employment, for example. The identity evolves over time. In any analysis of subcultures, we must be careful not to reduce the identity of a subculture to its outward sign and always relocate it back to its context as an expression of cultural negotiation between the group and the dominant culture in a given moment.

Counter-cultures, somewhat like subcultures, are based around a conscious questioning of the values of the dominant culture, but tend to be represented by a more coherent political position, one that often places them firmly outside of or 'counter' to the dominant culture. For example, the Hippy movement of the 1960s was an impassioned and informed response to, among other things, the Vietnam War, consumerism, reliance on technology and the work ethic. What differentiates the Hippy counter-culture from, say, a subculture such as the Skinheads, is the extent to which it intellectualises and articulates its position. This is, in part, a class difference. The Hippy movement was largely composed of middle-class members, whereas Skinheads and Mods were born of a disillusioned working class. However, whether sub- or counter-culture, an emphasis on dress and ritual is key to their representation within a society.

Rastafarianism is an example of counter-culture, combining elements of Christianity, African religion, and Afro-Caribbean culture. Rastafarians have distinctive codes of behaviour and dress, including the wearing of dreadlocks.

Culture

Introduction
What is culture?
All design is political: part two
Style and identity
Afterword

Afterword

**'Meaningful' is not the
same as 'full of meaning'...**

This chapter has looked at the ways in which various groups – sub- and counter-cultures – use dress and ritual as outward forms of resistance to the dominant culture. Normally, that resistance results in consensus because we live in a hegemonic society – a consensus about how we live our lives, dress, style our homes, work and play, and so on. We have also looked at notions of dominant and popular culture and the evolution of these in Western society in the latter half of the twentieth century.

In our postmodern society, we now enjoy an often fruitful blurring of distinctions between high and low culture, and many of us move freely between different categories that make the distinction pointless. Culture is the way of life, the rules and conventions that determine what's acceptable and what's not, and is expressed by the artefacts that result from, or challenge, it. Even cultural artefacts that are produced as a result of the so-called 'cultural industry', whether we view it cynically or not, have a meaning beyond what was intended by producers of those artefacts. The meanings and values of those artefacts are only realised at the site of consumption – with us, the members of society, a diverse and shifting, but nevertheless, coherent society.

Theory, as we said at the start of this chapter, is far from dry; it is the articulation of the workings of our everyday lives.

In this chapter we looked at:

Definitions of culture by Raymond Williams and of the concept of popular culture.

Critiques of mass culture by the Frankfurt School, which considered it to be passive and conformist, and as a means of keeping the working classes subservient.

The cycle of desire, consumption and disillusionment.

An explanation of the way in which advertising attaches meaning to banal things in order for us to fulfil our basic human needs through consumption and perpetuates the desire to attain more.

The idea that meaning is not invested in something at its creation, but when it is used. We looked at why mainstream films, novels can have more immediate value for many of us than more high-brow or designer examples.

The social dimension of consumption – we consume to acquire a sense of social identity and status, not just for the sake of consumption.

The definition of popular culture as a form of resistance to the dominant culture.

The term 'hegemony' to explain how the status quo of the various groups within a culture is maintained through a process of resistance, negotiation and acceptance. If a dominant culture is enabling and allows for dissent, it is less likely to be overthrown than one that enforces its ideals by violent means.

Consumption as a means of communication, and how this feeds the cycle of fashion and innovation in design.

The home as an example of how we customise our space. We asked if our homes are a true expression of ourselves, or if we are influenced by received ideas of taste and style, and meeting the expectations of others about what our private spaces should look like.

Fashion and the role of designers and manufacturers in determining how we consume their products.

The fashion cycle, based on 'Laver's Law' and the concept of 'bricolage' – how we use what is on offer to assemble our personal style.

Subcultures and counter-cultures as a form of resistance to the dominant culture in terms of dress and ritual. While subcultures tend to become assimilated, counter-cultures resist dominant culture more emphatically. But both use visual communication as a primary means of presenting their message.

The Practice

Introduction

Understandably, designers really struggle with the concept of the 'mass market', positioned as they are with one foot in the world of commerce and the other in the visual arts.

The arts have long been the home of individuals and groups working outside a society that also celebrates them. To work in the arts and design is perilous. It requires dedication, passion and drive. An artist must be prepared to embrace a more 'alternative' and insecure lifestyle. In fact he needs to extol it. He must have the will-power and drive to succeed. Work inevitably becomes a comment on and reaction against the status quo.

This chapter considers the mass market in relation to the consumer and asks how design negotiates between these positions. Mass production is a double-edged sword. It is democratising and therefore liberating, but it also threatens to eradicate difference and originality. Understandably, some designers are reluctant to perpetuate 'sameness' just because it sells.

But, ultimately, despite the frustrated creative considerations of the designer, design is a commercial enterprise, and who is qualified to pass judgement on public taste anyway, particularly in a relativist postmodern world? Design is constantly evolving, responding to changing consumer demands, and is subject to criticism from clients, end-users, peers and critics – none of whom uses the same criteria by which to judge it. Each has a different agenda. A client's focus is commercial success. Mass appeal is the main objective and clients are wary of producing anything too innovative or that deviates from pre-defined trends. And, for the designer, the more his or her work has mass appeal and is commercially successful, the less likely it is to be deemed 'worthy' in creative terms. Of course, the ideal would be to enjoy both, but often compromise works against it.

These issues are most relevant to the worlds of fashion and product design. Both straddle exclusive and mass markets. Both produce the ephemeral and the classic. Both can be manufactured by large- and small-scale producers, and both can be designed by teams and individuals. Can we extrapolate any truths from the experiences of fashion and product designers? How much do designers consider the real impact of their work as it leaves the marketplace and takes on a whole range of meanings for the consumer?

The practitioners

The practitioners who have considered the issues raised in chapter 2 work in fashion and textiles, and furniture and product design. Joan Farrer is from Britain and Shin Azumi and Tomoko Azumi are originally from Japan. The designers work in seemingly unrelated fields. But they are all acutely aware of mass market appeal and about satisfying the more exclusive end-users too. They all argue for the long-term environmental benefits of sustainability while recognising the unremitting voice of capitalism as it demands constant renewal.

Azumi, a London-based furniture and product design team, was formed in 1995 by Japanese designers, Shin Azumi and Tomoko Azumi. Azumi has covered all bases: producing inexpensive, sustainable and beautiful work for high street retailers, such as Muji and Habitat, while also designing for more high-end Italian, British and German manufacturers. They have designed installation pieces for exhibitions and whole suites of furnishing for hotels.

Despite the variety of its clients, Azumi has been uncompromising in producing quality products. Both designers focus on longevity and sustainability. They have distanced themselves from transient fashions and trends. Azumi designs classic pieces that will be manufactured for many years to come, and may ultimately acquire iconic status.

For them, design is about communicating quality of life. They want to produce everyday objects that enrich life. For example, a cup can be a beautiful vessel that keeps tea warm and feels satisfying in the hand or the mouth. It can function and be sensually pleasing at one and the same time.

Meanwhile, Farrer moved from overseas clients and concentrated on the UK mass market fashion industry, designing, among other things, Burton's best-selling men's jumper, and working as a consultant advising high-street retailers, such as Marks & Spencer and Tesco, on fashion and household trends. Like Azumi, Farrer has become increasingly interested in sustainability and how this will impact on practice, production and consumption in the future.

For the last ten years, Farrer has been involved in education as a visiting lecturer and is acting course leader in the School of Fashion Textiles at Central St Martins College of Art and Design, London, and between 2003 and 2004 was a senior research fellow. In her current research post in the School of Fashion and Textiles at the Royal College of Art, she is researching sustainability and smart textiles under the concept Con Science Clothing.

Joan Farrer

Biography

Joan Farrer was born in Cumbria, England, in 1956, and studied at Liverpool Polytechnic, graduating in 1978 with first-class honours in fashion and textile design.

The same year, Farrer joined Deryck Healy International, London, a major, inter-disciplinary design consultancy with an international portfolio of clients. In 1982, she and three colleagues founded East Central Studios Ltd., a design, colour and trend consultancy, working with Far Eastern and UK clients in the fibre, textile and fashion industry.

After the birth of her third child in 1993, Farrer founded her own freelance fashion, textile and branding consultancy, working for major UK retailers and their overseas supply bases.

In 1995, Farrer was invited to undertake a part-time research degree at the Royal College of Art and gained her PhD in 2000 investigating the global fashion textile supply and disposal chain in relation to issues of sustainability or people profit planet – a concept in sustainable business that states that all three are interrelated and that if one aspect suffers, all suffer.

In addition to her teaching posts with Central St Martin's College of Art and Design and research post with the Royal College of Art, Farrer continues to work as a design and strategy consultant for fashion retailers, non-governmental organisations, local government and research institutions. Her UK clients have included Arcadia Group, Conran Group, Courtaulds Fibres, FutureBrand, ICI Fibres DuPont, the International Institute for Environment and Development, International Olympic Committee IOC UK, Marks & Spencer, Tesco Stores, Virgin Stores and World Wildlife Fund for Nature.

Joan Farrer

In an industry preoccupied with the creation of desire and fixated with the new, Farrer has become a key proponent of sustainability and is concerned with raising awareness and evolving ethical approaches to design, production and consumption.

These life-size Con Science Clothing posters, with photographs by Clare Robertson, were part of the culmination of a three-year research project into fashion and modernity. Intended as faux fashion plates, the models are wearing clothing and accessories that raise issues about the supply chain and sustainability within the fashion industry.

Fashion and Modernity
CONsCIENCE CLOTHING
SHOOT

Kristien from Estonia
Central Saint Martins
third year BA fashion design
menswear student
wears

Hand woven cotton scarf Afghanistan. 10% of the world's pesticides and 25% of the world's insecticides are used to grow cotton. **Fake Watch Stockholm, Bracelet Portobello Market London.** There are *250 thousand child slaves* the fashion/textile/jewellery industry in India. **Bespoke tailored trousers, Oxfam London restyled by model.** *Britons throw away 1 million tons of clothing* each year equivalent to more than 3.5 times the volume of Canary Wharf Tower. Much consists of seasonal fashion items worn a few times and/or from non renewable resources. UK households throw away enough rubbish to fill the Albert Hall every hour. **Shoes Italy.** *One million containers of textiles clothing and footwear are shipped to Europe each year* much from unregulated global supply chains.

Concept: Joan Farrer Photography: Clare Robertson Production: Kristien Graphics: Landels

Fashion and Modernity
CONsCIENCE CLOTHING
SHOOT

from the UK
Central Saint Martins
second year BA fashion print student
wears

Second hand breakfast cereal Ad campaign T-shirt. One pound of cotton fibre is needed to make a T-shirt and uses ⅓ pint of pesticides. **Black cotton** Cotton growing covers 3% of the world's cultivable land much of which is in developing countries should this land producing food crops? **Cotton gym shoes Indonesia.** Michael Jordan's endorsement of Nike's running shoes earned him 20 million dollars which was more than the entire Indonesian workforce earned in the same year. **Leather holdall Morocco.** Leather processing and dye stuffs from unregulated countries can be carcinogenic to workers and wearers.

Fashion and Modernity
CONsCIENCE CLOTHING
SHOOT

Ralf from Germany
Central Saint Martins
second year BA fashion design womanswear
student
wears

Vintage military wool jacket Canada. Production of *wool* has significant *animal and farmer welfare issues*, pesticide sheep dips can affect nervous systems, electrical stunning for easy shearing can greatly distress the sheep, scouring can cause water table pollution. **Jeans Mexico.** A pair of cotton jeans travelled *19,000 global miles* from the farm to the factory to the customer and 5,000 miles more to the developing countries buying waste clothing via charity shops and clothing merchants. **Vintage charity shop shoes London.** Nearly 200,000 tons of clothing from *charity shops* and clothing banks are bought by entrepreneurs and sent to developing countries, it could be argued that this undermines their indigenous fashion textile industries.

Concept: Joan Farrer Photography: Clare Robertson Production: Kristien Graphics: Landels

Joan Farrer is well aware of how major retailers dominate the market. She is familiar with the different forms of cultural stratification used to assess demand and is clear about how design fits into the process. 'It's true that clothes, and in particular fashion, are not just about need; they're about belonging to the tribe, a club and sometimes about appearance of wealth,' she says. 'So, if you wear a Comme des Garçons jacket and you meet someone else who's wearing one, you know instantly that they know what you're about. The retailers have tapped into these needs and understand them too.'

Farrer was trained in fashion and textiles. Four years after graduating she and three colleagues set up a design, colour and trend consultancy working with overseas and UK clients. This is like being a fashion fortune-teller, and it is this, combined with her design experience, that gives her real insight: she sees both the retailer's and designer's position. 'For example, we would put together a concept package for yarn spinners,' she explained, 'making cloth out of their experimental yarn to show them what its fullest boundaries were. I worked with the first Teflon-coated cloth and the first Tencel yarn before the developments went fully to market; then it was really cutting-edge stuff. Further down the line we would create seasonal concept stories for fashion retailers too, but were hardly involved in the implementation. We often worked with both the CEOs and design teams in the early concept and design stages, then they took it on as their own.'

She went on to explain that although the understanding of demographics has changed, most major retailers still categorise along similar lines as those outlined in chapter 1, using the ABCDE system, for example. 'It was very clear cut. Now the boundaries are more blurred, the demographics have changed. With fashion design you really have to look at the audience. So Marks & Spencer's customers are, on average, aged 35–50. Tesco's can be 20–27. The criteria and considerations in designing for each are entirely different. Even within one retailer you'll have teams that work on different customer profiles and products. That's the same whether you're working for haute couture or the cheaper, high-street end of the market.'

Farrer is clear that fashion design is a commercial process driven by a retailer's Board of Directors and search for profitability. 'There's a dictate that comes from the company to the design team. Designers are not normally consulted on company strategy and very few make it to the Board. They're always one or two levels down in the management structure.'

'It's easier to drive it from the top down,' Farrer explains, but she adds, 'designers are still at the core of the industry as far as ideas and new product generation go; retailers do remember how much money designers are generating.' Alternative, experimental colour, pattern and/or silhouette ranges are usually developed alongside the more mainstream products. 'Every line will have its top experimental range and that's where there's a trial element. Retailers see from the sales whether they've been right with new ideas that may then be incorporated into the main ranges.'

Large retailers also enjoy contact with young, relatively unknown, own-label designers. 'The small guys will often make concept presentations to the big retailers. This, coupled with the extensive overseas travelling of the retailers' designers and buyers, ensures that the retailers are very aware of what's happening on that cutting-edge level too.' Youth-focused outlets like the British high street chain Topshop and Topman take this a stage further. 'Topshop really is a cathedral for young people who maybe aren't into real designer novelty or don't yet understand it or who could not afford it anyway. So, to capture the essence of a leading trend, Topshop may offer a short contract to young cutting-edge designers to advise them. Sometimes Topshop contract a design project at an art and design college offering prize money to the winners and making a small run of their collections for the flagship stores. They're a pretty sharp organisation at that tough competitive level of the market.'

Farrer is aware of the workings of the fashion industry and the demands and desires that drive it. Much of her consultancy work has involved trend forecasting for clients in the UK and Far East. Seasonal predictions of colour, mood and style are created well in advance and are often global.

Farrer's client concept presentation for Christmas home and gifts 2000/01 forecast the mood and key materials for that season and focused on opulence and tradition, inspired by the Spice Route. The catalogue pages show how the client translated this colour palette and inspiration into party wear and casual clothing ranges.

In Britain, the division between large and small enterprises is very clearly drawn. It has become so extreme that allegiances indicate a shopper's politics just as much as their taste or aspirations. This is not the case elsewhere. 'In Britain the market's driven by the five big clothing and supermarket non-food retailers and then you have the numerous – for want of a better title – Cool Britannia guys. Whereas, if you go to Italy there are one or two big retailers and then there's many more independent small chains that have maybe six or seven boutiques. They're family-owned and make their own design, manufacturing and pricing decisions, which means there is far greater variety of design on offer for the consumer. It's the same in Holland, for example. The UK is unique as the big retailers have bought out many of the small shops and manufacturers and therefore have economies of scale and control, but often at the expense of design individuality and range flexibility. That's why when you go to the high street sometimes everything is in the same colour or has a very similar quality.'

It seems almost impossible for designers in larger corporations to be 'alternative' or 'different'. 'The small guys are being led by something as well,' Farrer points out. 'Usually what's happening on the street and youth culture, the music scene, the clubs. If you go to Portobello Road on a Friday morning you'll see droves of designers and students at the second-hand and vintage shops and stalls looking for inspiration, so everyone in that case is looking at the same references.'

Farrer is unsure whether the public really want to be that different, and questions how many people overtly express themselves through their clothes. From the average teenager to an office worker, people are too insecure to break away from the codes of their own group. 'My kids don't want to be different. They want exactly what their peers have. You can see this wish to belong on other levels too; for example, if you look at a room full of guys in suits. The tie is different, the shoes are different, but the dress code differences are so finely tuned that the overall look is the same. The difference can be the positioning of a pocket on a red hood one season to the next, but it's still a red hood. There are very few pieces of clothing that are original, only maybe in the sports area, because of new, smart fabric developments and construction methods such as laser cutting and welding. The rest is just more of the same; it's the seasonal churn, the churn of decade upon decade.'

Designing for mass markets is not without its rewards and challenges. Farrer talks animatedly about the best-selling men's jumper she designed for Burton in 1997. 'There's a thrill in understanding the customer, creating newness and getting it right. One autumn we had a £19 million buy and full profit from a few successful lines of knitwear and that's really exciting.' No-one should run away with the idea that appealing to a mass market is so formulaic as to be easy. 'It's very pressured, the margins are incredibly tight and you have to be ahead of the game the whole time. Anyone can make a desirable range out of cashmere, but you try and make it out of 100% acrylic.'

Farrer has had good experiences working with high-street retailers, and particularly with Marks & Spencer. Working for colleagues David Davis and Stuart Barron and their brand agency, she developed the concept Autograph. 'Marks & Spencer had already been sponsoring individual designer names for some time purely from a philanthropic point of view. They took them on and nurtured them, giving floor space for their collections in top stores but it was fragmented,' she explained. 'M&S knew there were customers who would come into the store and pay more for these small designer label ranges and so decided to develop a more holistic approach to presenting the new designers that they wished to sponsor. Our brief was to amalgamate six or seven favourite well-known designers' labels and create a store within a store to house their collections. We put together a whole range of different looks all aimed at a sort of young Liz Taylor. Then we came up with a list of possible names and put together presentation boards that showed what the interior store might be like, the graphics and how M&S might present the products. The store within a store concept definitely increases footfall into the shop. You might go in to look at Autograph collections, but then buy socks, underwear, food – it could be termed a sort of loss leader that doesn't lose money.'

Farrer clarifies what she sees as the distinction between design for exclusive and mass markets. 'One is about the artefact and the other is about the process.' A limited edition bag uses the finest quality leather and 'all sorts of non-quantifiable, emotional pieces of input go into the piece – the delicate colour and feel of the leather, the colour of the gold on the buckle, the paper it is wrapped in at point of sale.' But the mass-produced equivalent is determined by 'how and where it is made, how quickly and at what price and how close to the original it can get without compromising profit. It's about the process of getting a saleable product on the table, whereas the other one is more about fine-tuning the aesthetic.'

During the last ten years, Farrer has turned her attention increasingly to the ethics of her business. She campaigns for greater consideration of sustainability and raises awareness of the inevitable waste generated by an industry so fixated by the new and design for obsolescence.

Her research started in the mid-1990s. She was in China putting knitwear into production for a big retailer and was shocked by the working conditions of the knitters there. 'I watched girls knitting on Dubied machines, some by candlelight. I noticed that they were standing in bare feet on duck boards. It was absolutely boiling hot and these lads came in with great big bins full of water and sluiced the whole of the knitting room floor, not because the girls were hot, but because you need almost 100 per cent humidity to knit fine silk on hand flat machinery. I thought, 'What is this all about... the business I'm in? Who is accountable?' That was the idea I went to the Royal College with – to investigate and relearn my business; having been in it over 20 years I realised that I had lost touch with it.'

The Provençal Blues presentation for Spring/Summer 2000 informed the colour and country lifestyle of this homeware range. Colour is an important sales device; using colour families allows for merchandise co-ordination, eye-catching catalogue spreads and in-store displays.

But this is not a simple tale of 'big means bad'. Farrer cites Marks & Spencer as 'the Oxford of retailers' from a more sustainable point of view. 'They've got such a history, they've always been such a paternal organisation. They had their own spinners, their own knitters, their own fabric makers, they were like the old Victorian industrialists who knew every factory and every part of the chain. They had a great loyalty to all their suppliers. Unfortunately, that changed when the power of the shareholder took effect in the 1990s. In 2001, I was commissioned to write a Marks & Spencer report called the Sustainable Textiles Research Project, which was incorporated into their corporate social responsibility programme. The report confirmed they had some of the best business practices at the time, without doubt. The company even appeared on the international Dow Jones sustainable index first as the best clothing retailer.'

The public seem to want ever-cheaper goods, but as Farrer points out this is not about real need and encourages mountains of textile waste. As debated in chapter 2, consumers are encouraged to develop a constantly renewed desire to consume. This may keep the tills ringing, but the long-term global damage could be profound. 'Quality retailers like M&S for instance find it difficult because the consumer wants cheaper and cheaper goods, but they are not about that philosophy. You could argue that Prada and Gucci are the most sustainable brands – if you buy a Prada shirt you're going to have it for five years, you're not going to wear it once or twice and throw it away as you would perhaps one from the high-street stores.'

Designers bear a great responsibility here. 'You could argue that they are central to that feeling for and creation of desire and therefore, by default, the ensuing waste,' says Farrer. For designers to make a difference they will have to rethink their role. 'The few designers who are political get a lot of press' says Farrer, 'like Stella McCartney and her non-animal substrate shoes or Katharine Hamnett's organic cotton. But it's a shame that the movement towards more sustainable products still has this slightly "brown rice" connection and is not sexy. There's also a group called the Ethical Fashion Forum that has just appeared. They are all very young and squeaky clean and determined to make a difference. The problem is that there isn't yet a homogenous ideology or theory that guides these groups.'

'What I try to convey to my clients and design students is that the future of design may not be about markets necessarily or even customer needs. It is about materials, production, design innovation and integrity in relation to a sustainable future. If designers were confronted with a room full of leather off-cuts, what are the challenges in creating a desirable product, for instance? The challenge for design in the future will be about innovation, limitation of materials and designing for disassembly... a fantastic new direction for design to go.'

This example of Farrer's 'design room presentation' is for Burton menswear, Spring/Summer 1997. Photocopied and collaged inspirations from a range of sources are used to create style studies that the in-house buying team uses for range co-ordination and trend information.

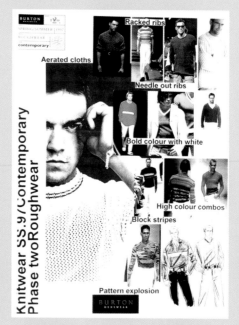

These fabric swatches are from Autumn/Winter 1996 and show the working colour palette to which all products in this range must adhere. Swatches are used by buyers for colour-matching when sourcing and dyeing fabrics. Retailers often test colours in small capsule collections before including them in larger ranges.

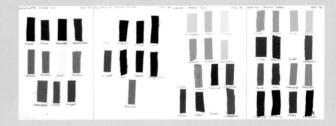

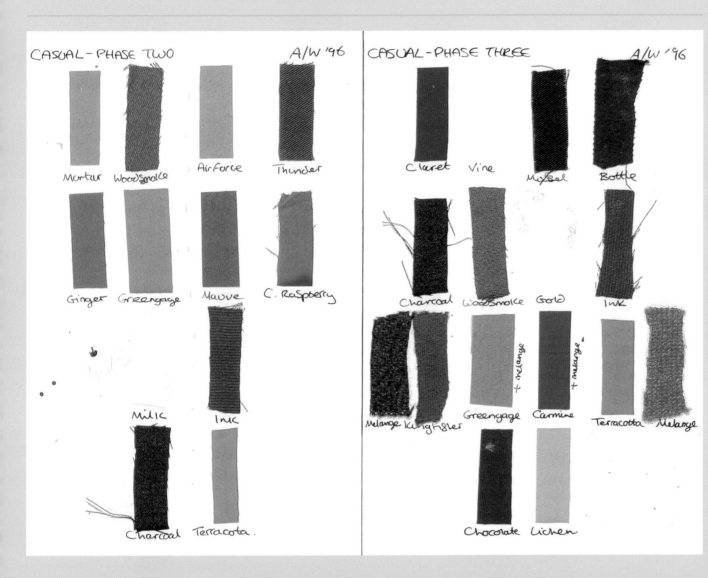

Successful high street fashion design is measured in sales, and a range of merchandising methods are utilised to attract the customer. Fair Isle patterns and stripes are useful colour vehicles to show the full palette within a clothing range. They allow for tied-in co-ordinated items and provide a strong focal point for displays.

Farrer disputes the notion that making affordable, popular clothing for a mass market is an easy task and has enjoyed this challenge herself. She is proud of designing a best-selling jumper (far right), the core-product in a nautical collection for Burton, 1997.

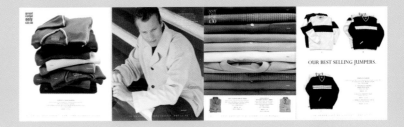

Shin Azumi and Tomoko Azumi

Biographies

Shin Azumi was born in Kobe, Japan, in 1965, and studied product design at the Kyoto City University of Arts in Japan, graduating in 1989 with a Bachelor of Arts. He worked for three years for NEC in Japan as an in-house designer before taking a Masters degree course in industrial design at the Royal College of Art in London, which he completed in 1994.

Tomoko Azumi was born in Hiroshima, Japan, in 1966. She took a degree in environmental design at the Kyoto City University of Arts and graduated in 1989. She worked for several architectural practices in Tokyo during the following three years and then took a Masters degree in furniture design at the Royal College of Art in London. She graduated in 1995.

Shin and Tomoko formed a team and founded their studio in London in 1995. For ten years they worked together in furniture, product and space design.

Their first show was at 100% Design in 1996, where they exhibited a range of tableware and flexible furniture. They continued to launch new work at design trade shows until their last showing at the Salone Satellite exhibition of Salone del Mobile in Milan in 1999.

They have worked for international clients, including Authentics (Germany), Lapalma (Italy), Habitat (UK), Hitch Mylius (UK), Guzzini (Italy), Isokon Plus (UK) and Muji (Japan).

Their first piece of exhibition design formed part of Tectonic at the Crafts Council, London, in 2000. The installation was called Misty Lounge. In it, Azumi explored the integration of space and objects and introduced the use of dramatic lighting.

In 2004, Azumi was nominated for the shortlist of the Jerwood Applied Art Prize for Furniture Design and showed its work in the show at the Crafts Council. Work shown included the Lem bar stool, Comb chair and Donkey 3. Lem was awarded Product of the Year by the FX International Interior Design Awards, 2000, and it was produced by Lapalma in Italy. The Comb chair is the latest chair produced with an experimental plywood structure by Benchmark Furniture. Donkey 3 refers to the original Penguin Donkey and Donkey Mark 2, and is produced by Isokon Plus.

In 2005, Shin Azumi and Tomoko Azumi opened independent design studios: A Studio and TNA Design Studio.

Shin Azumi's and Tomoko Azumi's work is characterised by their belief that objects should always give pleasure, both functionally and aesthetically. They hope their work will subtly change the way the consumer behaves in his or her environment for the better.

left to right, top to bottom
From the Snowman Salt and Pepper Shakers, 1999, that unusually only require a gentle tilt, to the Orbital WorkStation, 2003, an award-winning approach to school furniture, this selection of work demonstrates wit and versatility.

The Cross Tables, 1999, have storage beneath and can be joined together, whilst the Muji crockery, 2003, is an interchangeable set of black and white items. Azumi developed simple platform structures for the Spa at London's Mandarin Oriental Hotel, 2000, to help create an appropriately calm atmosphere.

Shin Azumi and Tomoko Azumi have dealt with a number of the theories raised in chapter 2, but they are keen to maintain some distance. Their work has managed to be aesthetically refined, rational and functional whoever the audience and client may be. They have avoided considering audience categorisation by seeing their work as part of a much bigger and more stable picture. 'What we do is design something that is very sensible, lasts and touches on the real truth of people's needs,' explains Shin Azumi. 'Of course on a superficial level we can adapt to fashion, like changing the colour of a seat depending on a trend, but functionality is not about trends. If I can find that kind of truth then I am happy.' Both designers have quiet confidence in the philosophy they have developed and this enables them to be equally trusting of their audience. 'We don't know,' says Tomoko Azumi, 'but I think the product itself will choose the person who will buy it, so I'm pleased when I see it in any sort of location.'

It was in this spirit that they both approached the text. They considered notions of high, low and popular culture objectively. Perhaps cultural differences go part-way to explaining their approach to design. 'We come from a very democratic country,' says Shin. 'I'm actually surprised you still think about the class system in Britain. I guess in product design it is about the different meanings an object may have. A precious, one-off object is maybe supposed to be exhibited in a museum or in some rich person's place. But what I'm really interested in is producing objects that are purchased in mass-quantity.'

Neither designer considers that broad market appeal and mass production need compromise quality and result in inferior goods and uniformity. 'Mass production often implies a cheaply made object in this country [the UK], but it's not necessarily so. Think of computer products. They are sophisticated and use precise technology that needs precise engineering.' Shin continues: 'My intention is not to create a special object. My intention is to produce daily objects. Our Lem bar stool, for example, is made to be mass-produced and sold. It's not necessary for individuals to buy one because they are in public places, so all people can feel them or enjoy them. My preference is to share that kind of joy with the maximum number of people.' Tomoko picks up a cup they have designed as part of a set commissioned and sold by Muji stores throughout the world. 'This costs £5,' she says, 'this is for everyone.'

For both designers the design process offers a great challenge. Unit costs and ingenious and expedient use of materials are some of the factors that will determine the eventual design. Shin explains that for him originality is not about aesthetics. 'It's about original thinking and original use of materials or technology. Working cleverly within the constraints of the human body.'

Azumi designed Table = Chest in 1995. It's a chest that can be quickly converted into a low table – an ingenious design that embodies much of their approach to flexible furniture design.

Azumi has produced various items for Habitat. Originally only in the UK, this high-street outlet now has stores in France and Germany too – all selling contemporary furniture and household goods. The products have to be easy to assemble, normally by the end-user, and reasonably priced. 'We had to think about these aspects quite seriously,' says Shin. '[Habitat] is mass market but we have tried to design things that don't look cheap. Sometimes completely different design solutions come out of the price limitation. Design is a puzzle. There are always lots of different considerations. Once I have understood the needs that have to be addressed, then I can start to design.'

When asked if there is any status attached to owning their work Shin and Tomoko look mystified. 'Status is as much related to where something is sold and how much it costs as to the name of designers,' says Tomoko. 'But in our field this is not as powerful as in fashion. People don't buy, for example, that bar stool, for this season. It stays with you for longer. It means that you don't buy it just because of status, you want to live with it.' Shin Azumi and Tomoko Azumi want people to buy their designs because of the product not their name. 'I design quite a lot of products where the designer's name isn't shown,' adds Shin. 'People buy some of our work because it's unbranded and sold by Muji, so it's anonymous.'

Communication is at the heart of both designers' work. Shin explains: 'For me design is communication with other people. So, if we can communicate with people what we think is important through an object we have designed then that is a good end.' Tomoko continues: 'We want our objects to be comfortable for your body and your eyes, to not be very noisy in your environment.' To this end Shin and Tomoko try to be playful within their design. They distil their ideas until results are simple, yet surprising. Shin corroborates: 'It's tactile and physical and spiritual as well. Spiritual is a dangerous word, but I guess we mean that we hope our work can lift the spirit.'

For neither designer does mass production equate to cheap and therefore throwaway. Neither sees themselves as producing work that will become part of the 'cycle of desire' discussed in chapter 2, because longevity and sustainability are their primary considerations. Shin mistrusts audience categorisation, arguing that it leads to mediocrity. 'You can sell quite a lot of products using these methods, but you can't create excellence or objects that last ten years or more,' he explains. 'Longevity is important. Otherwise we're just destroying our environment too much.'

'There's an awful lot of superficial work in product design,' he continues. 'A lot of it is driven by the constantly changing technology. Models change every year, or even half-year, and the design has to change slightly too to keep up the demand for the new. It's a bit sad. We too are part of the circulation of money. We cannot deny capitalism. We are living in that world. But we can try to be careful.'

The excessive use of polycarbonate in the mid-1990s is a prime example of a fashion-led abuse of materials. 'The introduction of polycarbonate for the first iMacs was a new way of using that material. But then suddenly everything looked like an iMac, regardless of appropriateness,' Shin explains. Tomoko tries hard not to be susceptible to this kind of influence, but is also aware of the power of zeitgeist. 'I don't want to be influenced by all of that. But people do think in a similar way at a similar time.' Inevitably both Shin and Tomoko know that their work will be copied. 'The copied products are not the same quality as ours,' they explain. 'So, we just see it as a kind of honour.'

Both designers see design as a symbiotic process. They are open to influences from all around them, drawing reference from everyday life as well as from sub- and counter-cultures. Tomoko considers favourably how the perception of their work may change according to how its owner may use it. 'If someone buys it because they love the functionality of it and then they take it home to somewhere less appropriate then that's fine. I don't care if very simple objects are surrounded by ornaments. They are personalised that way so I'm pleased. We've had work in galleries positioned next to a Buddha head from China and at other times I've seen it in a messy living room. People receive it in many different ways – this is good.'

Tomoko acknowledges, however, that design success relies heavily on meeting like-minded people – particularly clients. 'We have been lucky enough to meet people who share our feelings,' she explains. Shin adds: 'We have to make things that we like; we have to be able to present our work feeling comfortable with our idea.'

Public acclaim 'is a big wow', says Tomoko, but Shin is concerned about how their objects are marketed and sold. 'If an object is not presented in the proper way to the proper audience, I feel it is a mistake. I remember seeing the Authentics products presented in a souvenir shop in Japan in a Tokyo station, with a souvenir of Tokyo, together with a very kitschy object. This is a well-designed, functional object. It's not a kitschy object. This is a misunderstanding of how to put a product into a shop.'

Despite the focus on function and simplicity, both designers refer more to postmodernism than modernism. 'Somebody was saying to me the other day that my work looks very influenced by modernism but what I'm really doing is disassembling the functionality of the object and then putting it back together in my own order. This is quite a postmodern approach,' explains Shin. 'When we were studying we saw lots of postmodern work,' continues Tomoko, 'but we were not part of the generation that made it, we were too young.'

Tomoko sees her methodology as open to change. 'I don't believe that there's one right way to work,' she explains. Shin adds: 'I'm always being influenced by lots of bits and pieces from all over the place and I try to generate my own methodology. My attitude is to question everything. If I have a fixed attitude or fixed direction, at some point I will start questioning myself again. I'm always moving.' By disengaging with preconceptions, Shin Azumi and Tomoko Azumi have managed to find a truth all of their own.

Azumi is interested in designing objects that last and 'touch on the real truth of people's needs'. This does not preclude working commercially for the mass market. This set of crockery was commissioned by Muji and is sold in its stores throughout the world. 'This is for everyone,' Tomoko says.

right
Azumi was approached by Isokon Plus to design the next in the iconic 'Donkey' family. A prestigious commission, the result was Donkey 3, 2003. As with previous Donkeys it combines shelving with a low table and makes reference to both the original Penguin Donkey of 1939 and Donkey 2 designed by Ernest Race in 1963.

below
ShipShape, 2003, has two obvious functions; a magazine rack and low table. Produced from bent plywood for Isokon Plus, it is as strong and versatile as its companion piece Donkey 3.

Azumi has designed a variety
of different pieces for the
Italian furniture company
Lapalma, including the ZA range
of stools, 2003–04. These
stack inventively and come
with corner pieces so that they
can be grouped in curved
as well as straight formations.

The Lem bar stool, 2000, was commissioned by the Italian manufacturer Lapalma. It is a high stool with a swivel seat and adjustable height. The seat and footrest are comfortably distanced apart whilst the sinuous line that connects them gives this stool its characteristically refined form.

The Music Tube 2000 is a space
inside the boutique and café
Restir in Kobe, Japan. The area
is used as a corridor to the
café, but also acts as a display
for the selections of CDs
that are for sale. Visitors can
stop and listen en route.

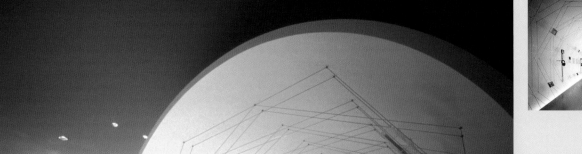

below

In the late 1990s, Azumi, inspired by an everyday object, designed a series of Wire Frame furniture. The production method, spot welding, is used for supermarket shopping baskets. The bench is also reversible, forming a chaise longue when upside-down.

right

Misty Lounge, a room installation for the Tectonic exhibition at London's Crafts Council, 2000. The boundaries between space and objects are blurred by an ingenious use of light and shadow, transparency and opacity. Visual tricks are created by 1,500 bungee cords combined with items of Wire Frame furniture and illuminated by wall and hanging lamps.

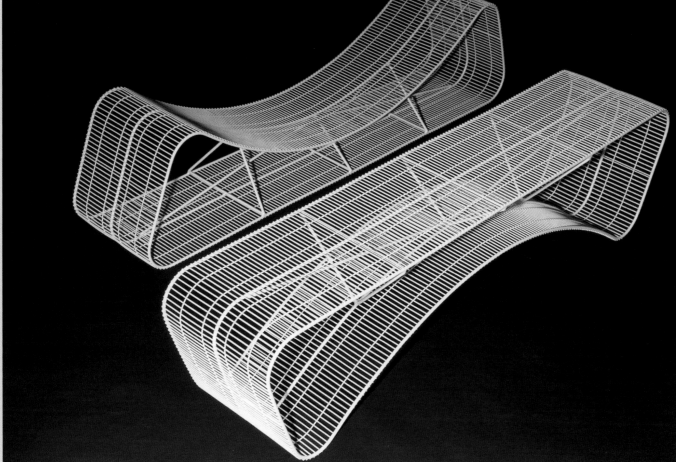

Visual communication

Front matter
01 Communication
02 Culture
03 Conflict
End matter

02 **Questions in summary**

01 How have you 'socially consumed' culture recently? What meaning did it have for you and those around you?

02 Can designers work outside 'culture' or must they always be a part of it?

03 Shin Azumi and Tomoko Azumi's designs are mostly bought by people who have no knowledge of who they are, and therefore without designer status in mind. Do you think this is ideal or should we have auteur designers?

04 How have Shin and Tomoko Azumi's experiences of and opinions about designing for the mass market challenged your own views about mass-market design?

05 What do your choices of clothes and furniture and homewares say about you? Do they represent the 'real' you, or the person you aspire to be? Looking at photographs of yourself from the past, how has your appearance changed and what were the influences that determined it?

ISBN-13: 978-2-940373-09-3
ISBN-10: 2-940373-09-4
90000>

9 782940 373093

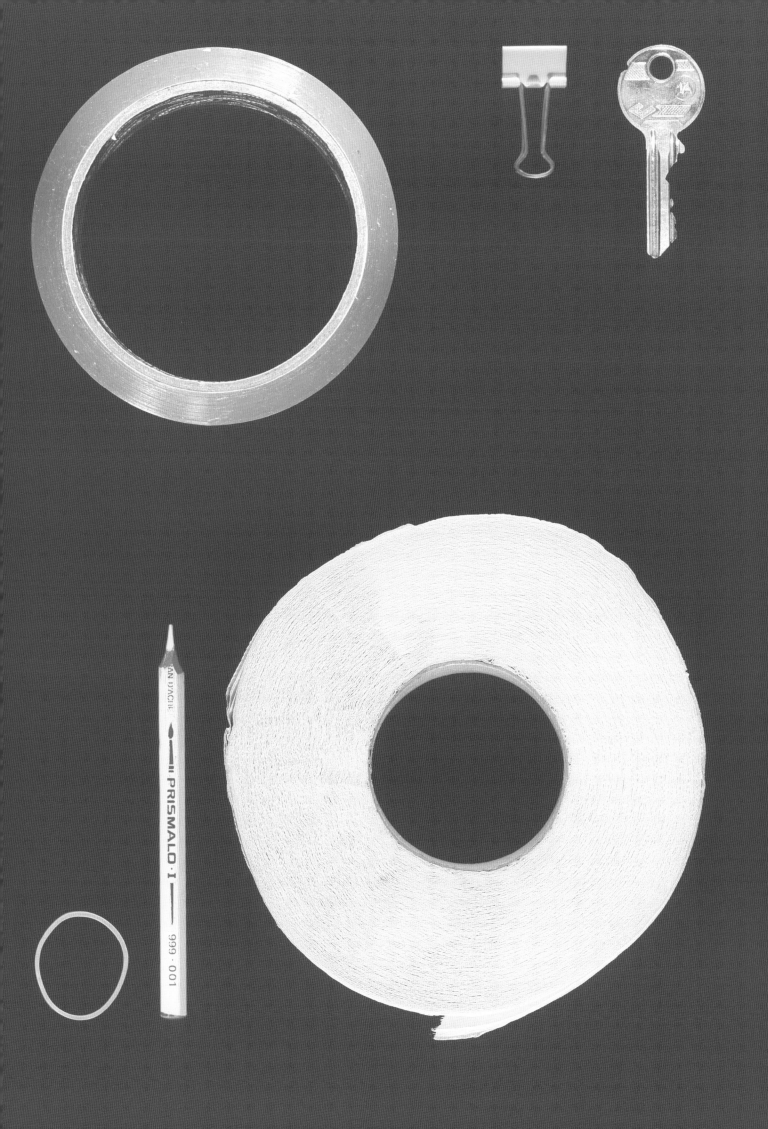

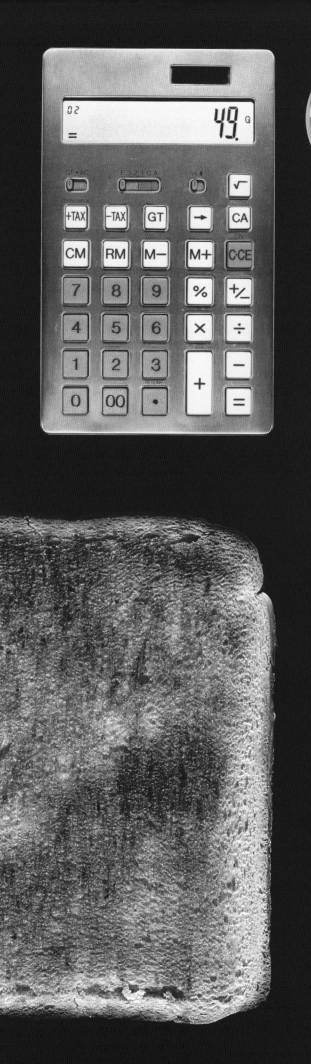

Visual Communication

Front matter
01 Communication
02 Culture
03 Conflict
End matter

03   Conflict

Aims of chapter 3

This chapter's essay introduces you to:

An explanation of why objects can become valued for their form out of proportion with to function.

The increasing political awareness of designers and the problems they face translating this into practice.

The potential of the democratisation of design to affect professional designers.

An analysis of how understanding the workings of professional design demystifies it and affects its status.

These key theories are then given real-life industry responses by two international designers:

Erik Spiekermann explains how the theory of political activism can conflict with the harsh realities of commercial practice. He also discusses how his lack of orthodox design training left him open to criticism from some of his peers.

Emmi Salonen describes her frustration with her education, which she believed failed to engage with her intellectual and political concerns. She recounts her experience of trying to practise her beliefs and the problems she faced before finally being happy with her activities as a designer in the community.

Conflict

Introduction
All design is political: part three
The political designer
Design under threat?
Afterword

The Theory

Introduction

**Form versus function:
Styling as communication**

In chapter 1, visual communication theory was examined to show how design works with readily available and culturally accepted signs and symbols to produce simple design. This 'function over form' approach is a feature of a great deal of successful visual communication where the message comes from 'above' – advertising, politics and the media, for example.

In chapter 2, one of the items we discussed was how, for example, fashion, can be one of the means by which we resist those messages – how they can be appropriated and adapted from 'below', the democratisation of design. We also looked at the issue of form and function. Interestingly, in terms of furniture design, our practitioners demonstrate how form and function can coexist harmoniously as one – and with great success, providing one of design's biggest challenges.

In this chapter we examine the rise of the 'political designer', someone who uses design to effect political and cultural change. Political designers create messages that can be powerful, creative and innovative. While worthy, their work can be exclusive and their audience limited. This 'political' design is oppositional rather than propositional, and while the potential for peer approval is high, and many designers find themselves being lauded as style icons, we look at how much scope there is for designers to effect political or social change. Political power comes from changing people's minds, not confirming those of the people who already agree with you.

Popular culture shows how style can be used as an effective means of visual communication and protest. For design-led political resistance, the aim for designers might be to emulate some of the methods of those they oppose. This means adopting and subverting the style of advertising and other media in order to create new and effective forms of communication.

Producing politicised and creative work can be a process of struggle and frustration for the designer. If designers really want to communicate the need to change the way we live, one of the most effective ways to do this is to rethink what it is that people want. Designing for social needs, for everyday life, is one strategy available to the political designer.

However, there is another site of conflict in the world of visual communication, one that occupies a significant part of the design industry and education: What is design? What's it for? Who's in control? Is the designer subservient to the needs of the client and the marketplace, or should designers assert their autonomy?

Keywords in this chapter

Culture jamming
The act of subverting the messages presented to us by government, media and corporations with the intention of creating an alternative meaning, or exposing the hidden 'truths' behind the original message.

Mac Monkeys
A pejorative name for designers who can 'do' design, but lack the understanding of the effects or responsibilities that come with the practice. 'Mac monkeys' are seen as the product of a focus by education on skills rather than a deeper understanding of design, arguably brought about by government and industry pressure to provide trained workers.

WordArt Man
A pejorative name for an amateur designer who produces work using the relatively unsophisticated tools available to him, and against whom 'professional' designers find themselves competing for work. The term derives from the clip art found in Microsoft Word.

Conflict

Introduction
All design is political: part three
The political designer
Design under threat?
Afterword

All design is political: part three

Design for the real world

39
See *Design for the
Real World: Human Ecology
and Social Change* by
Victor Papanek (London:
Thames & Hudson, 1985).

Designer and educator Victor Papanek (1927–99) was a strong advocate of the design of products and tools that were socially and ecologically 'responsible'[39]. He identified a tendency in Western cultures to produce products that are potentially harmful, extravagant, or just plain useless.

Although in his lifetime he was often lampooned by those he criticised, many of his ideas have come to be viewed favourably. Papanek, for example, criticised our over-reliance on cars and excessive use of massive and ecologically unsound aircraft, instead proposing the development of a new generation of airships. In more recent years there has been a revival in interest in these, particularly for use as alternatives to satellites (for telecommunications in cities and for anti-terrorist radar platforms, for example).

Papanek wrote about the loss of vision in design education, and believed that this began in schools that prized surface details over functionality. Papanek famously designed a radio that could be made from an old tin can, powered by burning a wick in fat. Intended for use in developing countries, it was to be made for, and adapted by, the people who used it. The idea was derided on aesthetic rather than technical grounds – proving his point exactly. Arguably, the design may have failed to catch on due to the commercial pressures involved to produce something more sophisticated.

Trevor Baylis's wind-up radio transformed the lives of the poor in Africa, and has become a design classic elsewhere. While the 'design' focuses on the mechanism that powers it, the styling of the body of the radio has been kept deliberately economical, in both senses of the word.

No matter where we live, we are bombarded by information and appeals to our desire to consume. Who controls what information we are given? And how can we resist the advertisers?

A similar example reinforces this point. In 1993, British inventor Trevor Baylis caught a programme on the BBC about the spread of AIDS in Africa, and learned that radio was often the only available means of communicating the information required to prevent it. However, the need for batteries and electricity made radios too expensive or too difficult to use. Baylis went on to design a wind-up radio that took a great deal of time to develop. Even when the technology was perfected, it was only manufactured once it looked visually pleasing enough to be marketable, despite its urgent benefits.

Why are we talking about Papanek and Baylis in the context of visual communication? The radio examples are important because they show that good design does not necessarily depend on primarily aesthetic considerations. Papanek saw that overly decorative or extravagant designs are often unnecessary, sometimes unsafe and ill-thought-through, being designed to foreground style rather than function. The radios of Papanek and Baylis were not meant to be visually appealing items, but to facilitate the production of an important communication device – in the case of Baylis's radio, communicating life-saving knowledge. However, if something works well, it often has its own kind of beauty as the aesthetic is not superficial, but intrinsic.

Vehicles that travel across rough terrain are a vital tool in farming and in countries with little infrastructure – but their high fuel consumption and damaging effect on inner-city roads makes them a poor choice for town driving. Yet SUVs (sports utility vehicles) are becoming more and more popular, a status symbol rather than an essential mode of transport. Is this a case of how products become meaningful at the site of consumption? Of how the status of form supersedes function?

Conflict

Introduction
All design is political: part three
The political designer
Design under threat?
Afterword

Herman Miller's Mirra chair is a good example of Papanek's ideal of design that serves a useful function without damaging the environment. As well as being designed with the comfort of the user in mind, it manages to look good. But it is also environmentally friendly. Its designer claims that 96% of its materials are recyclable. However, this and many other 'green' products still require users, local government and waste disposal companies to be supportive.

Fruit comes ready packaged by nature. Wrapping apples in plastic, below, is wasteful. The desire of supermarkets to display 'perfect' fruit and vegetables has a damaging effect on farmers who have to throw away apples that are the wrong shade of red or have an irregular shape.

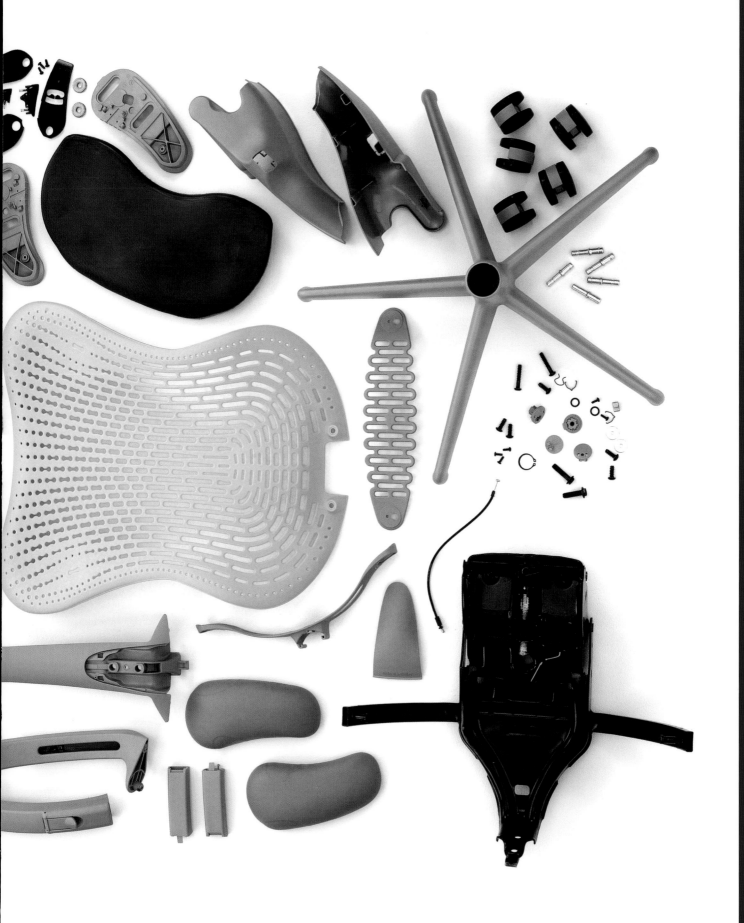

Conflict

Introduction
All design is political: part three
The political designer
Design under threat?
Afterword

The political economy of signs

Papanek's disdain for form without (or before) function is understandable. It is certainly something designers should bear in mind, and it is a view that has gained a greater degree of sympathy in recent years. Neo-Marxist theory, for example, ties the desire for socially aware design to using style as a form of visual communication, which links the three chapters of this book together.

Classic Marxism theorises that in capitalist society we promote 'exchange value' over 'use value'. Marxism claims that the system is inverted and fundamentally flawed.

French philosopher and postmodern theorist Jean Baudrillard argues against this reductive viewpoint. He has looked at how people relate socially and has found that one of our prime motivating factors in life is to find a sense of meaning and of 'place'. This is similar to Maslow's hierarchy of human need – we are driven by a quest to feel autonomous and in control, but also to belong to a social group. And this is why we use objects such as furniture, clothes and even radios the way we do. Their 'use' value may be large or small, or even non-existent, but often they possess properties that make them far more valuable in other ways.

Let's return to the flowers as discussed in the section on semiotics in chapter 1 by way of an example. In that section we discussed how a bunch of flowers could have a different meaning depending on whether they were given to a lover, mother or sick relative. The meaning (love, affection, well-wishing) is invested in the flowers' status as a gift[40].

For the person receiving the flowers, the meaning is invested not only in the status of the flowers as a gift, but possibly as a symbol of his or her relative importance, too, particularly if they are displayed for others to see. Yet for the person selling the flowers, they have no meaning at all beyond that of commodity value. And the flower itself has no inherent cultural value beyond those imposed upon it.

What is happening here is that the gift of the flower moves quite freely between four different states (what Baudrillard refers to as 'areas of logic') and in each of the areas it has a different value. These are summarised in Table 4[41].

Table 4
The political economy of the sign.

Areas of logic	Object status
Utility	Instrument
Market	Commodity
Gift	Symbol
Status	Sign

In chapter 1 we looked at how flowers can change their meaning depending on their context. In the political economy of the sign, objects can move freely from being plants to commodities to gifts and status symbols (see Table 4).

Baudrillard's idea helps to explain something that many critics find frustrating: why do we focus on the apparently trivial, such as surface detail, at the expense of function? Because, theorises Baudrillard, we use objects in many different ways and the usefulness of a radio, for example, is not just in its ability to receive radio transmissions, but in its value as a symbol of status; its value as a gift and its value as a commodity.

Our use of objects as gifts and status symbols is not simply a product of capitalist society or mass culture, but of our need as human beings to communicate socially; and visual communication provides the most direct means of doing that. As Baudrillard puts it: 'Human beings do not search for happiness; they do not search to realise equality; consumption does not homogenise – it differentiates through the sign system. Lifestyle and values – not economic need – is the basis of social life.'[42]

Papanek's definition of 'social need' might be at odds with Baudrillard's, but his tin can radio is a perfect example of how function and form interrelate. Baudrillard would applaud the way in which such a functional object is appropriated and individually styled to personalise, be given an identity. The challenge for the designer inspired by people like Papanek is to produce artefacts that are useful, safe and ecologically sound – and socially desirable. Design may not always be fundamentally about aesthetics, but it is often the clinching factor in getting profound ideas accepted.

40
A gift to someone acts as a sign of affection or love. It is not inherently meaningful beyond its function. The more the gift resonates with the meanings attached to it – the 'thoughtfulness' of the gift – the greater it acts as a symbolism of love or affection. The value is in the symbols, not the gift itself.

41
See *For a Critique of the Political Economy of the Sign* by Jean Baudrillard (Telos Press Ltd., 1983). For a good introduction to Baudrillard's fascinating, complex thought, see *Routledge Critical Thinkers: Jean Baudrillard* by Richard J Lane (London: Routledge, 2000).

42
Fifty Key Contemporary Thinkers: From Structuralism to Postmodernity by John Lechte (London: Routledge, 1994) p 234.

In Marxist theory, capitalist society places exchange value over use value. Shops are full of cheap bread that stays 'fresh' through the use of anti-bacterial and preserving agents. The rise in popularity of home bread-making machines in recent times suggests we want better bread, but what do we really value: a better-baked loaf or the status of the 'homemade'?

Conflict

Introduction
All design is political: part three
The political designer
Design under threat?
Afterword

The political designer

Culture jamming

43
See *Culture Jam: The Uncooling of America* by Karl Lasn (New York: Eagle Brook, 2000). The Adbusters website can be found at www.adbusters.org.

For the designer, the ideal must be to produce design that reflects the needs of the producer without betraying the needs of the consumer and his or her own vision. It is naive to believe the designer can be responsible for every eventuality – and he or she must accept that the end-user might well appropriate his or her message. This is no bad thing. It inspires debate and reflects a healthy, democratic process. Part of the success of a piece of art is the way it can be appropriated and reinterpreted to subversive ends.

Nowhere is this seen more clearly than in the work of culture jammers who attempt to subvert the messages of the major producers, whose practices are deemed to be unethical. Prime targets are tobacco firms, clothing companies that employ third world labour, and the beauty industry that promotes an unhealthy obsession with being thin and which relies on animal testing. Cigarettes and alcohol are advertised by associating smoking and drinking with escapism, in the form of sport, tropical islands and other visible signs of wealth and desirability. Yet claims are made that the poorer the neighbourhood, the greater the incidence of this type of advertisement. Not only are the products sold on a false promise, but addictive, unhealthy and expensive items are peddled to those who are the least able to participate as consumers.

Rather than publish literature attacking the companies and advertisers, culture jammers acknowledge that there is power in subverting them by turning their messages to advantage – in a very graphic way. The work of the culture jammer inspires debate. Alongside other forms of protest it can be a powerful means by which opposition can be made directly to the producers of culture and to the captivated consumer alike.

Culture jamming can be subtle and witty or direct and confrontational. Either way it provides a vehicle for protest.

Three tactics used are known as 'adbusting' or 'subvertising'. The first, vandalism of advertisements, a kind of graffiti, is the least effective, because it is opportunistic and lacks the sophistication favoured by culture jammers. The second subverts the meaning of the advertisement by subtle cosmetic alteration of the imagery or text, often using precisely the same materials and techniques to produce sophisticated messages that require a double-take – a second or third reading gives greater impact. The third, and most direct, involves defacing the ads to highlight the underlying 'truth' – in an advert for fashion, for example, faces of models are blacked out with markers to make them look like skeletons, for example.

Although not the first or only proponents of culture jamming, the Canadian-based Media Foundation and their Adbusters magazine are the best known[43]. As well as disseminating current thinking and the best subvertisements, they also run campaigns such as 'Buy Nothing Day', which takes place the day after US Thanksgiving. From their website, visitors can download Buy Nothing Day paraphernalia, including a voucher that excuses the recipient from having to buy a gift in return. Most recently, the Adbusters site has begun selling 'Black Spot' sneakers, deliberately void of any logo (except the black spot) and made without recourse to 'slave labour'.

While powerful brands are an easy target for the culture jammers, it shows the potential power behind this form of protest. It can be an important form of non-confrontational and intellectual protest. But its very accessibility might begin to dilute its message as it becomes integrated into the mainstream or 'hegemony'. At least it invites public reaction.

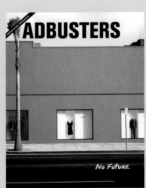

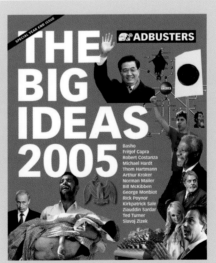

Adbusters, once an underground magazine, has gradually found a regular place in mainstream newsagents. As it becomes more successful, does this dilute its message? Is it in danger of simply being a badge that people wear to communicate their allegiance? Or do its readers act on its contents?

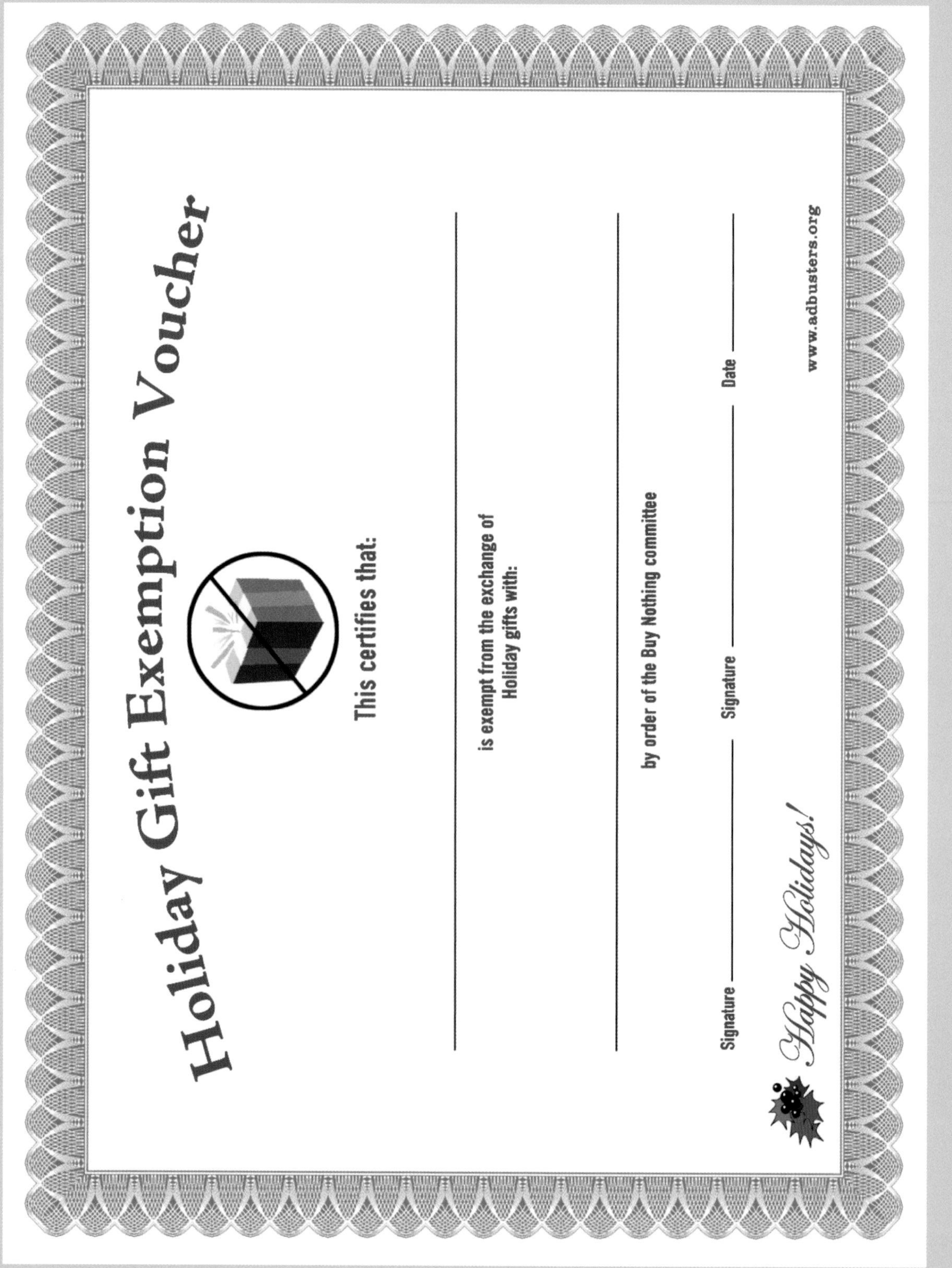

Conflict

Introduction
All design is political: part three
The political designer
Design under threat?
Afterword

Holiday Gift Exemption Voucher

This certifies that:

is exempt from the exchange of
Holiday gifts with:

by order of the Buy Nothing committee

_____ _____
Signature   Date

www.adbusters.org

_____
Signature

Happy Holidays!

ESCAPE

from
Calvin Klien

Examples of Adbusters' 'subvertisements'. The Holiday Gift Exemption Voucher, part of the annual 'Buy Nothing Day'. In the US, attempts to run TV ads explaining their values were banned by networks for being 'anti-American'. Free speech is only 'free' for those in power. This case is interesting for how an anti-capitalist stance is also considered to be unpatriotic.

ABSOLUTE END.

The No Logo generation

44
No Logo by Naomi Klein
(London: Flamingo, 2000).

The publication of Naomi Klein's *No Logo*[44] in 2000 marked a new phase in the design-led challenge to the power of corporations to control economies and pursue 'unethical' practices for the sake of profit. *No Logo* is one of those books that simply to own it means something. Ownership of *No Logo* has become a statement of belief. The number of design students who own a copy points to the emergence of a new generation who are turned off by the very things that once attracted students to study design. They are less interested in conspicuous branding and more interested in pursuing a more radical form of design.

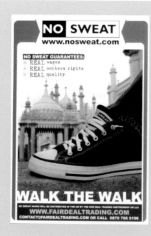

The logo-less black spot sneaker is an example of how adopting the tactics of the large corporations can be powerful. There is no fear of culture jamming becoming a brand in its own right – brands in themselves are not bad as long as they act responsibly. These shoes show it is possible to manufacture desirable and affordable goods without exploiting workers.

The Visual Display of Quantit...

NO LOGO NAOMI KLE...

EYE NO. 45 VOL. 12 AUTUMN 2002

EYE NO. 47 VOL. 12 SPRING 2003

Paul Rand

Steven Heller

CHRIS WARE — COOL STUFF — OPENTYPE — HOOFD...

/Mapping

color

Roger Fawcett-Tang
William Owen

VOLUME 4

Trademarks & Symbols Of The World: EUROPEAN

An illustrated guide to graphic navigational systems

ed. Teal Triggs

communica...

Exactitudes

VOLUME 2

Trademarks & Symbols Of The World: DESIGN E...

KUWAYAMA **TRADEMARKS & SYMBOLS**

JON WOZENCROFT **THE GRAPHIC LANGUAGE OF NEVILL...**

EXPERIMENTAL LAYOUT

IAN NOB...

Phil Baines & Andrew Haslam **Type & Typog...**

Deborah Wye **Thinking Print**

MetaDesign Design from th...

above
Naomi Klein's *No Logo* sits on many shelves. Critics derided its success, claiming that it had become a brand in itself. Except that the whole point of the anti-branding movement is to expose the shameful practices supporting our brand obsession, not to do away with branding altogether.

left and right
Direct action can take many forms, from vandalising adverts and logos to making different kinds of public protest.

Conflict

Introduction
All design is political: part three
The political designer
Design under threat?
Afterword

First Things First

There is an undoubted shift in attitudes within a new generation of design students which, as they graduate and begin to work in the creative industries (in whatever capacity) may grow into a paradigm-changing movement. But it would not be the first attempt to do so. In 1964, designer Ken Garland produced the 'First Things First' (FTF) manifesto, which reacted strongly against the consumerist culture prevalent in Britain at the time, and which advocated a humane dimension to design practice. It was signed by over 400 designers and championed by Tony Benn, who that year became Postmaster General in the Labour government, a role that involved overseeing the communications industry in the UK. Benn ensured that the manifesto was published in the *Guardian* newspaper, guaranteeing exposure beyond the already converted.

The 2000 revival of FTF challenged the notion of graphic design as being conservative and reactionary and foregrounded its responsibility not to promote immoral industries and practices. Although aimed at graphic design, the sentiments of the manifesto reverberated throughout all fields of design.

Table 5
Text of the original First Things First Manifesto, 1964.

We, the undersigned, are graphic designers, photographers and students who have been brought up in a world in which the techniques and apparatus of advertising have persistently been presented to us as the most lucrative, effective and desirable means of using our talents. We have been bombarded with publications devoted to this belief, applauding the work of those who have flogged their skill and imagination to sell such things as:

cat food, stomach powders, detergent, hair restorer, striped toothpaste, aftershave lotion, beforeshave lotion, slimming diets, fattening diets, deodorants, fizzy water, cigarettes, roll-ons, pull-ons and slip-ons.

By far the greatest effort of those working in the advertising industry are wasted on these trivial purposes, which contribute little or nothing to our national prosperity.

In common with an increasing number of the general public, we have reached a saturation point at which the high pitched scream of consumer selling is no more than sheer noise. We think that there are other things more worth using our skill and experience on. There are signs for streets and buildings, books and periodicals, catalogues, instructional manuals, industrial photography, educational aids, films, television features, scientific and industrial publications and all the other media through which we promote our trade, our education, our culture and our greater awareness of the world.

We do not advocate the abolition of high-pressure consumer advertising: this is not feasible. Nor do we want to take any of the fun out of life. But we are proposing a reversal of priorities in favour of the more useful and more lasting forms of communication. We hope that our society will tire of gimmick merchants, status salesmen and hidden persuaders, and that the prior call on our skills will be for worthwhile purposes. With this in mind we propose to share our experience and opinions, and to make them available to colleagues, students and others who may be interested.

(who signed the original manifesto) and Emmi Salonen offer their own thoughts on the realities of putting the theory into practice later in this chapter.

first

things

first

A manifesto

We, the undersigned, are graphic designers, photographers and students who have been brought up in a world in which the techniques and apparatus of advertising have persistently been presented to us as the most lucrative, effective and desirable means of using our talents. We have been bombarded with publications devoted to this belief, applauding the work of those who have flogged their skill and imagination to sell such things as:

cat food, stomach powders, detergent, hair restorer, striped toothpaste, aftershave lotion, beforeshave lotion, slimming diets, fattening diets, deodorants, fizzy water, cigarettes, roll-ons, pull-ons and slip-ons.

By far the greatest time and effort of those working in the advertising industry are wasted on these trivial purposes, which contribute little or nothing to our national prosperity.

In common with an increasing number of the general public, we have reached a saturation point at which the high pitched scream of consumer selling is no more than sheer noise. We think that there are other things more worth using our skill and experience on. There are signs for streets and buildings, books and periodicals, catalogues, instructional manuals, industrial photography, educational aids, films, television features, scientific and industrial publications and all the other media through which we promote our trade,

society will tire of gimmick merchants, status salesmen and hidden persuaders, and that the prior call on our skills will be for worthwhile purposes. With this in mind, we propose to share our experience and opinions, and to make them available to colleagues, students and others who may be interested.

Edward Wright
Geoffrey White
William Slack
Caroline Rawlence
Ian McLaren
Sam Lambert
Ivor Kamlish
Gerald Jones
Bernard Higton
Brian Grimbly
John Garner
Ken Garland
Anthony Froshaug
Robin Fior
Germano Facetti
Ivan Dodd
Harriet Crowder
Anthony Clift
Gerry Cinamon
Robert Chapman
Ray Carpenter

Commercial reality

As laudable as the aims of the FTF might be, for many it is difficult to support and implement. FTF was signed publicly by a group of leading designers, each of whom was arguably established and in a position to choose their commissions and turn work down. For some, supporting the FTF might have meant risking damage to their careers. However, the manifesto at least challenges the producers and the consumer, as well as other designers, to consider ethical questions in relation to design, which is worthy in principle, if slightly more troublesome in practice.

Selecting work on grounds of principle might appear to contradict the ethos of modern design education, the design industry and the design press, which seek to attract big-name corporate clients above the apparently less prestigious design advocated in First Things First. Do students who pursue a career in ethical design risk damaging their careers by narrowing their specialism? Or do they help to open up the debate within the field of design? Must choosing to design ethically mean sacrificing commercial opportunities? The list of guest speakers from the industry invited in to give talks to students of design betrays the apparent need for some commercial bias. The challenge for design as an 'industry' is to pursue aesthetic solutions and social responsibility at one and the same time.

Design is misunderstood and an easy target. This story from UK tabloid the *Sun* (August 6, 1996) contains several inaccuracies and misconceptions. First, their mock-up of the new logo is wrong, and secondly the cost is off the mark. But the money spent was not just for changing the logo – it applies to the research that was undertaken to discover how the BBC (a publicly-funded broadcaster) was perceived by its audience and what it needed to do to ensure its viewers continued to consider its service value for money. These values, encapsulated in the new logo, channel idents and other ways, were then applied to all areas from video covers to outside broadcast vans.

While critiquing the ways in which public money is spent is laudable, when newspapers (and the political party whose spokesman is quoted here) spend money on design, cost rarely seems to be an issue, presumably because it is considered to be an essential financial investment.

Does this article reflect public opinion or is it media hype? What value do we, and should we, place on design? Is it largely invisible to the general public or is it a subject for public debate?

M TO
NGE
LOGO

B B C

TO THIS

How Corporation insiders say the new BBC logo could look

Outrage over waste of our licence cash

By NICK PARKER

THE BBC is to spend an estimated £5million of licence-payers' cash making a tiny change to its logo.

The three sloping boxes of the current emblem will be straightened and the coloured lines beneath dropped.

But the minor adjustment will mean major changes to all the Beeb's stationery, screen graphics and paint jobs on vehicles.

And the enormous cost, which experts estimate could soar to £15million, sparked outrage last night.

OBSCENE

A BBC source said: "Most staff here view this as an obscene waste of money.

"Changing the corporation's logo won't improve the quality of its programmes. It's scandalous.

"How can they expect the public to hand them more licence money when they spend it like this?"

David Shaw, Tory MP for Dover and Deal, said: "This sounds like the most appalling waste of licence-payers' money. There are

Continued on Page Two

Conflict

Introduction
All design is political: part three
The political designer
Design under threat?
Afterword

Design under threat?

45
Respected academic Umberto Eco, is, for many, more famous for his novels, most notably *The Name of the Rose*. Eco suggests that the process used to decode a text must be different from the encoding process (see chapter 1) if the reader differs in any way (particularly socially) from the author. In mass communications, Eco argues, aberrant readings must therefore be the norm.

In chapter 2, we discussed how, far from being strictly the domain of professional designers, visual communication is something in which many of us can actively participate. We produce meaning as an everyday occurrence. Designers have a role to play in this; they produce the products that are used to produce the meaning: the clothes, the furniture, the magazines and the buildings, etc. But it is clear that what happens to a design once it is in the public domain and begins to be used, is out of the control of the designer or the designer's clients. In many ways, this is a fascinating aspect of being a designer; the way in which the consumer uses the designer's work may be at odds with what was originally intended – indeed, as Italian academic Umberto Eco pointed out, this tendency towards 'aberrant reading', far from being the exception, is in fact the rule[45].

But in the past few years something more has started to happen to design as part of everyday life; technology has opened up the practice of design to the home user or the amateur designer. We touched on this earlier in the book, and it's worth examining what is going on in a little more detail. This is because it poses something of a challenge to the expertise of designers and for visual communications.

The idea that good design has to be produced by professionals to professional standards, is plainly untrue – just look around you and see how much information is successfully conveyed in ways that wouldn't win any design awards, but score highly in the effectiveness stakes. 'Vernacular' design is another form of visual language. It may be crude, but it works.

We're all designers now!

International television schedules have been dominated recently by a plethora of TV programmes in which ordinary people's homes are taken over by teams of designers and transformed or, in the words of one UK show, 'rescued', from the excesses of their owners.

The trend does not stop at housing. A glut of personal makeover shows in which people are given a critical dressing down over their clothing choices and taught how to dress, walk and talk to get dates are clear examples of how the role of design and visual communications has never been more embedded into public life. Everyone and everything is available for re-styling. Never before has it been more democratic, because in all of these shows the idea is to 'educate' the participants and the viewers in the 'secrets' of good design and good taste, and the viewers sometimes get to vote too! Even when the expert presenters take the view that they are rescuing people from their style nightmares, the underlying point is to give simple advice to help us, the viewers at home, avoid similar mistakes.

The direction and formatting of these TV shows are emulated in print. Books and magazines covering the same subjects have been around for a long time, but in recent years the process has perhaps been felt most keenly in the graphic design profession. While the discussion that follows is focused on this area of design, its implications are equally pertinent to other areas of design, too.

Conflict

Introduction
All design is political: part three
The political designer
Design under threat?
Afterword

Opportunities to design our living spaces are all around us. While it democratises design, it has an effect on the design profession and its integrity. This is perhaps more true of graphic design, as fashion and product designers have always accepted that their work is going to be treated as a commodity.

Conflict

Introduction
All design is political: part three
The political designer
Design under threat?
Afterword

The Mac generation

Before the advent of the Apple Macintosh in 1984, graphic design was seen as a skilled and time-consuming job that involved teams of people, from the designers who came up with the concepts to the artworkers who produced the line-art, rubbed down the Letratone and cut everything out with a scalpel, before giving it over to the paste-up artists who stuck it all together using cow gum and spray mount. Each role required different skills and different backgrounds: humanities graduates were likely to drive the conceptual side, and trainees and apprentices worked more closely to the side of production.

It would be wrong to say that the Mac changed all this, but it certainly hastened a process of amalgamation between the 'creative' and 'artworker'. This has a lot to do with the development of qualifications in graphic design and a greater emphasis on training, a phenomenon that extended to all areas of the economy throughout the late twentieth century. In the UK, for example, the expansion of higher education mirrored a desire by companies to reduce their responsibility (and costs) for training their own employees, which placed the burden on taxpayers instead[46]. The transfer of responsibility for training graphic designers is no doubt partly responsible for what Lorraine Justice, author of *The Big Squeeze*, discussing the widespread introduction of computing technologies into graphics courses, calls the 'squeezing of the curriculum'[47], which led to the current focus on skills rather than theory, and on breadth rather than depth. The educational and technological focus has shifted from specialisation to generalisation, and from understanding and ensuring effectiveness to a focus on aesthetics. As a result, many people seem to believe that visual communication is entirely composed of the 'surface' of life and, to a degree, that anyone can be a designer.

We see a consequence of this in the representation of design in the media. It is not unusual for rebranding exercises to be judged in the press (see pages 144–145), especially when the organisation involved is a public body such as the British Council or government department, or one which is under fire for making staff redundant or providing a poor service (train companies, airlines and the like have all suffered from this in the past). This is, of course, how it should be. Public money should be spent judiciously. And the taxpayer has every right to know. However, in large part, rebranding ultimately saves money by increasing business, and the cost includes far more than just the design. This places the designer in an uncomfortable position in relation to his or her perceived role in having to provide, unfairly perhaps, justification for the work.

This article asks the experts how graphic design works. Graphic design is a discipline, like other fields, and training is essential.

The general public is well-served in its attempts to become fully-fledged designers by the mass of magazines and step-by-step books that demonstrate how to 'do' design using cheap or free software and a home PC. This is a relatively small investment. People have been designing their own clothes and decorating their own homes for centuries, but now they are also producing their own magazines, posters, greetings cards and websites. It is not uncommon for graphic designers to find themselves outbid for a job by someone with no training, who promises to do something for virtually nothing over the course of a weekend armed with nothing but a copy of Microsoft Word and built-in clipart. Under-cutting costs makes the 'home' designer, or what is popularly known as 'WordArt Man', potentially appealing.

46
For a fuller discussion of this trend see *Does Education Matter? Myths About Education and Economic Growth* by Alison Wolf (London: Penguin, 2002).

47
The Big Squeeze by Lorraine Justice (New York: Allworth Press, 1998).

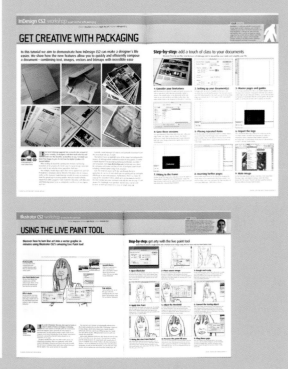

Designers might read these magazines for quick ideas or as a refresher on skills. But can the main audience for this publication – WordArt Man – armed with a PC and some cheap software, be a designer by night? Is that acceptable to both the client, the public and professional design?

All design is political: part three
The political designer
Design under threat?
Afterword

No: more rules

But let's stand back for a moment. Should we really worry if people are happy to put up with amateur design? The concept of what is 'good' taste is dependent on what sociologists call an 'illusio', a 'truth' established by producers of culture with a vested interest, but which is irrelevant to others. There are many examples of 'bad' design, where the designer has employed clichés, made errors in the kerning, chosen poor colour combinations and opted for hackneyed typefaces.
If a high-profile campaign for a major company produced compromised design (and it happens), it's bad news for design. But if home-produced design is local, for individual or small-scale purposes, function and economy may be paramount. And who's to say it's bad? It has its own market.

The answer is that good taste is important primarily to the dominant cultural elite, but for the consumer it may be less significant as long as it works. The person reading the sign or buying the packet of food or scanning the newspaper is undoubtedly aided in the task by clear communication, but at what point does clarity require some measure of style to facilitate it? When does design stop being communication and start being Design with a capital 'D'? The irony of the situation is that – as typified in some of the interviews earlier in this book – many designers reject the 'rules' that aid communication only to find them replaced by a new set of rules that promote the 'auteur' designer above the content.
It is in the interest of design and education to maintain the illusion that aesthetics and taste are very important, because it is the mastery of the aesthetic – 'good' design, if you like – that mark out 'experts' from 'amateurs'. The 'no more rules' mantra is perhaps better phrased as 'no: more rules'. This works as long as the aesthetic aspect of design doesn't become style for its own sake. And as long as it doesn't go too far in supporting exclusivity for designers.

48
See chapter 1.

49
Economic capital is increasingly a requirement for access to education as well – an important prerequisite for entry into many spheres of life.

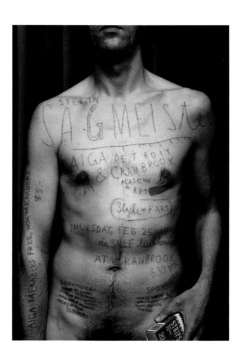

Is graphic design guilty of succumbing to the trappings of the art world by foregrounding affect over effect? Or will, as we suggest in chapter 1, today's entropic design become tomorrow's redundant design?

The field of cultural production

The field of cultural production is, as we saw in chapter 2, often divided between high and low or popular. French sociologist Pierre Bourdieu calls high art 'autonomous' art, and low art 'heteronomous'. Heteronomous art is mass-produced for a mass market – the sort of novels produced for reading on the beach while on summer holiday, movies such as *Bridget Jones's Diary*, mass- produced prints sold in furniture shops, advertisements, food packaging, high-street fashion, etc.

The demand for such products is external – the designers, writers and artists did not produce them as the result of some inner impulse – and the forms they take are predetermined. 'Innovation' and 'creativity', as the terms are often used, are not features we would expect to find here. In communication theory, these products could be said to be highly redundant[48], while the Frankfurt School would deem them to be unchallenging and inferior, designed to keep people sedated and intellectually oppressed.

What is missing in heteronomous art is what marks out autonomous art: creativity, innovation and imagination. In communication theory, autonomous art is highly entropic, and the Frankfurt School theorises that it is challenging and liberating. The audience for autonomous art is a cultured, socially mobile one; one which understands the concepts and the techniques employed by the designer (for example, intertextuality, self-referentialism and irony). These are art critics, collectors, the social and cultural elite and, importantly, other artists. Not, it should be noted, 'ordinary people'. For producers of autonomous art, if the viewer does not 'get' it, they are branded with the stigma of shame for not living up to the art.

Heteronomous art is concerned with economic capital (buying and selling) while autonomous art is concerned with social and cultural capital – it is exchanged for status, respect and authority. However, as Bourdieu points out, economic capital is often a prerequisite to social and cultural capital (it costs money to enter the 'cultured' world, and if you have enough money you can overcome your cultural naivety)[49] and artists swap their symbolic capital for hard cash when they sell their work or are wined, dined, and patronised. Bourdieu insists that autonomous art exists within a market, even if the market is purely symbolic in the form of reputation, as reputation brings status, and status drives the pursuit of distinction that defines you in relation to everyone else.

The designs that designers celebrate amongst themselves are, of course, aimed at that particular audience. But it can be argued that the desire amongst designers to win this peer approval removes them from the realities of 'real world' graphic design, creating the gap that is filled with amateurs.

Conflict

Introduction
All design is political: part three
The political designer
Design under threat?
Afterword

Is design art?

Increasingly, the design press is indistinguishable from the art press, reflecting a fusion of the two.

That art and design have become fused (or, some might say, confused) has not been without its critics. Victor Papanek took a characteristically forthright and critical view of the trend for design to be characterised as art: 'The cancerous growth of the creative individual expressing himself egocentrically at the expense of the spectator and/or consumer has spread from the arts, overrun most of the crafts, and finally reached design. No longer does… the designer operate with the good of the consumer in mind; rather, many creative statements have become highly individualistic, autotherapeutic little comments by the artist to himself'[50]. He raised an important point. For many commentators, this period has now been superseded. Stephen Heller recently asked Milton Glaser, 'How do you feel about the self-indulgent, designer-as-artist-above-all-else era of graphic design that we just passed through?' 'Thank God it's over', was his response.[51]

Fine art can have a primarily aesthetic rather than functional or intellectual purpose, and is considered to be a statement of the artist's vision rather than simply a way to make money. With art, the act of interpretation is important, but, as we saw in chapter 2, there is usually a 'correct' interpretation. Being able to make the correct reading and, importantly, to share that successful reading with others, is part of the artistic discourse that contributes towards the field's distinction – if you can do it, and have command of the language to do it, you are 'in'.

Another feature of art is that its practitioners are widely perceived to exist separately from, or in defiance of, the 'real world', and to possess a certain mystique that is reinforced by an outspoken rejection of the 'rules', an eccentric appearance, moodiness and other traits. The Frankfurt School described art as 'social magic'. Being someone who creates art or someone who appreciates art, sets you apart as gifted and sensitive, and as having good taste.

But the definition of art as we know it is a fairly recent phenomenon, as John Carey notes in his book *What Good Are the Arts?*[52]. Up until the Enlightenment, the word 'art' was used to describe any skill and an artist could be a hunter, a statesman, a blacksmith, a carpenter, a tanner or any manner of things. Artists as we now know them were simply part of this vast group of craftsmen and tradesmen (they were, of course, almost always men). Only since the eighteenth century has there been a shift in definition, with art and artists becoming synonymous with the pursuit of some abstract 'truth'. 'Art for art's sake' is a term often heard in this context. Indeed, art began to be described in almost religious terms, and those who pursued it were seen as following a calling or vocation, their 'skill'. The role of the artist enjoys a much less stable identity today.

It could be argued that what was once true of art is now true of design. Why is this? One answer, without judging whether design should or should not be seen as another form of art, is that it is a natural response to a perceived threat to its status from at least three sources: the denigration of the role of the designer in visual communication by its commentators as illustrated in chapter 1; the widespread growth of amateur designers armed with newfound skills as outlined above; and the privileging of design studies as a degree subject rather than a vocational skill.

It could be argued, based on the ideas of Pierre Bourdieu, that the design industry's response to these pressures has been to create, or recapture, a sense of distinction, the set of discourses which emphasises shaping and nurturing 'natural creativity'. It has, in other words, reinvented itself as a form of art, borrowing the trappings of mystique (the tortured lone designer in pursuit of aesthetic truth), the canon (the list of great designers and a chronological design history), the language, the accepted wisdom of taste – what is good design and bad design – and the gatekeepers (the critics, the star designers and the teachers) who determine between them an exclusive body of knowledge.

These factors have arguably led to a rejection of practice (how to 'do' design) and the critical theories (how design 'works') in favour of the pursuit of design for design's sake, and a language with which to discuss it that excludes those who do not understand it or cannot or do not wish to participate.

Circular logic

If this is true, then the end result is a source as well as a site of conflict between different parties. Not only is design in conflict with itself, but it feeds the very conflict the move towards distinction set out to counter. Design is often profoundly misunderstood by the end-user and media. While most people take their clothes to a specialist to have them dry-cleaned, get a builder in to add an extension to their home and a plumber to fix the central heating, many amateurs think they can 'do' design, because the process has been demystified and is much less exclusive, much less something that only an elite few can create and judge. It is a 'chicken-and-egg' situation: the more amateur designers encroach upon professional expertise, the more designers redefine what it is that makes them designers. And the more they shift the definition, the more the amateur decides to do it for himself.

As this book seeks to demonstrate, the visual world and its producers, its users and its designers, are engaged in a heated debate over the status of design – who has ownership of it, who is qualified to do it, and how we receive and interpret it. It is in a period of evolution, and requires more developed and rigorous understanding.

50
Design for the Real World: Human Ecology and Social Change by Victor Papanek (London: Thames & Hudson, 1985) p 40.

51
The Graphic Design Reader by Stephen Heller (New York: Allworth Press, 2002) p 3.

52
What Good Are the Arts? by John Carey (London: Faber and Faber, 2005) p 7.

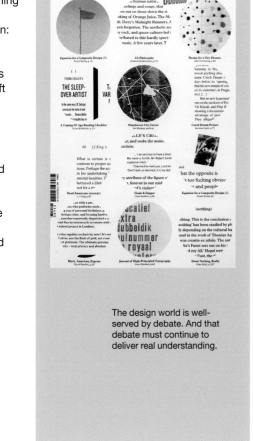

The design world is well-served by debate. And that debate must continue to deliver real understanding.

Conflict

Introduction
All design is political: part three
The political designer
Design under threat?
Afterword

Afterword

Beneath the surface

It may seem odd to say this, but whatever your view of the discussion in this chapter, it should be clear that design is not simply a visual medium; it is a social and, as we have identified, a political one. It just happens to be most apparent visually in the messages sent to us by commerce, media and government, and the subtler but equally important messages we send each other in our everyday practices.

Like an iceberg, 90 per cent of visual communication is hidden beneath the surface. And, just like an iceberg, it is the invisible 90 per cent that provides the raw power of visual communication.

So, there we end this overview of some of the key ideas that are involved in the study and understanding of visual communication and its relationship with design. Undoubtedly, like some of the practitioners interviewed for the book, you will disagree with some of it. Hopefully some of it will have challenged your own position on this subject.

I hinted at the end of chapter 1 that while some people consider theory to be a mystification of practice, rather than a tool for disseminating or supporting it, I believe that theories help us to appreciate our practice with more depth and resonance. Ultimately, your response to what we've outlined in this book might be to suggest a theory of your own, based on your own thinking and experience – as some of the practitioners we've interviewed do. But be careful in distinguishing between a theory and an opinion. The difference between a theory and an opinion is that a theory is supported by empirical evidence. The next stage is to work out how you can put your own informed opinions to the test and turn them into a sound theory.

Finally, remember that this book is by no means the last word on anything. We hope to have whetted your appetite to look at visual communication in more detail, and pointed you in the direction of alternative sources that will extend your knowledge even further.

In this chapter we looked at:

The argument put forward by theorists such as Victor Papanek, that designers have a moral responsibility to improve the lives of those who use their designs.

Criticisms of capitalist society that it promotes the value of aesthetic objects over functional ones.

An explanation for why we consume – to create a sense of identity – which theorist Jean Baudrillard saw as an essential aspect of our existence as social beings.

Attempts by designers to become politically active, and the way in which their work can be appropriated by culture jamming, for example.

The *No Logo* generation of designers who reject the impact of unethical branding and globalisation, and the 'First Things First' manifesto – which was conceived in the 1960s and revived at the turn of the twenty-first century.

How practical it is for designers to reject many of the concepts and ideologies that might enable a more ethical design culture. And we asked what pressures were being put on students to bow to, rather than resist, commercial forces.

The relationship between the design industry and the public, particularly given the growth in design handbooks, cheap computers and software, and the compromised respect for design as a profession. The rise of 'WordArt Man' was offered by way of an example, but so too was the response of some designers that arguably widens the gap between designers and the public.

The work of sociologist Pierre Bourdieu to explain why designers have responded in this way, suggesting that the movement of design into the world of art, complete with its own language, traditions and heroes, is an attempt to regain a sense of mystique that has been lost over the past few decades.

The Practice

Introduction

Here is a moral dilemma. As a politically aware, socially engaged graphic designer, do you:

remind your client that in order for their new publication easily to fulfil the criteria of the disability legislation the type size needs to be increased

or

not say anything because smaller type will result in an elegant design that you consider to be more appropriate and that will therefore be more successful?

As a professional designer you are aware of the legislation and have read the guidelines that specify minimum type sizes and preferred colour usage. Also as a professional designer you know that the intended audience will respond positively to a more refined design solution. In your experience access is not just about big type anyway. White space is also a valuable commodity. Less is more, after all. More space means less visual clutter, greater clarity and therefore easier access, but the guidelines don't often mention this. Whose responsibility is it to raise these issues and who ultimately decides?

Next dilemma. Do you talk to your client about sustainability, recycled paper and more environmentally friendly printing? Do you make sure that all ethnic groups, for example, are represented in the images? Do you refuse to carry out the project if they are not?

Reference has been made throughout this book to the relationship between politics and design. Our practitioners have all agreed that the two are inextricably linked. As Michael Bierut said: 'Much, if not most, graphic design is about communicating messages, and many of those messages are intended to persuade. This places its practice clearly in the realm of politics.'

Chapter 3 is about politics and designer responsibility. It asks, to whom are designers responsible – the client, the end-user, the world... themselves? Surely it is irresponsible to take a client's money and not apply oneself professionally to the task? But what if the client is misleading the end-user in some way? What if the environmentally friendly paper that you are advising should be used is more expensive and considered by the end-user to be less desirable? What if the client then goes bankrupt and you don't get paid? This is not really about design, it is about defining an approach to life.

What is a 'political' graphic designer? Is it someone who is producing manifestos, protest materials and sabotaging the work of opponents? This is certainly active demonstration, but it is also a very simplistic understanding of what is meant by 'political'. Political engagement is as much about what you don't do as what you do do. So, what about those who seek to change society by disengagement – designers who are particularly discriminating about their clients based on careful evaluation of their intended message?

Is there an aesthetic or an approach to the process of design that can clearly be identified as political? All design decisions can be informed by a political position, but as our next practitioners demonstrate, the results can range from a slogan on a badge to a piece of information design.

Chapter 3 asks if designers could take a more active role in changing people's approach to design by questioning the association of beauty with money and value. It argues that designers have inadvertently bought in to these notions by valuing form more highly than outcomes determined by analysis of function.

Forget for a moment the notion of 'form follows function'; what we really need to do is determine the function of design. Can it and should it be to make the world a better place? Can the designer be as aware of these concerns when designing a cup that keeps tea warm, sits perfectly in the hand, doesn't spill liquid as you drink from it and has a sculptural quality, as when designing a hospital signage system that gets a paramedic into Accident and Emergency more quickly? That's for you to decide....

The practitioners

The two practitioners who have considered the issues raised in chapter 3 are both graphic designers: Erik Spiekermann from Germany and Emmi Salonen originally from Finland and now working in New York. They are 30 years apart in age, and, thus far, their political inclinations have taken them on very different paths. Salonen is an idealist who is not afraid of active protest. Spiekermann signed the First Things First manifesto in 2000 from a position of pragmatic idealism. He has no expectation that the manifesto will be implemented. He is aware and accepting of the reasons why not, but still considers it right to ask the questions and provoke debate.

As a graphic design student at the University of Brighton in the UK, Salonen was frustrated by her contemporaries' disinterest in politics. She applied to Fabrica, the Benetton Research and Development Communication Centre in Italy, hoping to find a forum in which to combine politics with further creative studies and practice. Fabrica's best known output is *Colors* magazine. Founded ten years ago, under the direction of Tibor Kalman, it is based on the conviction that all cultures have the same value and that the richness of diversity should be protected.

Fabrica selects young artists, designers and researchers from all over the world and invites them to participate in a range of communication activities, in cinema, photography, graphics, design or music, as part of *Colors* magazine or within the interactive department. Learning is through hands-on involvement in real multidisciplinary projects.

In 2002, after her year at Fabrica, Salonen returned to the UK, working for two years at Hoop Associates, a design practice specialising in work for the voluntary sector. She has subsequently worked in New York as a graphic designer at Karlssonwilker.

Erik Spiekermann is best known for his rational approach to typography, his font design and large-scale information design projects, coupled with his sharp wit and incisive mind. Spiekermann is refreshingly objective about graphic design and graphic designers. Having studied history of art he came to the profession as something of an outsider and he remains a more objective observer.

In 1979, he founded MetaDesign, now Germany's largest design firm. Projects included the design of the new passenger information system for the Berlin public transport corporations and corporate design programmes for Audi, Skoda and Volkswagen. As someone whose specialism is information design, Spiekermann has been able to apply a more humane approach to the corporate world.

In 2000, Spiekermann withdrew from the management of MetaDesign Berlin. The following year he was commissioned to redesign *The Economist* magazine in London, and has now set up a new design practice, United Designers Network, that is currently designing the corporate design programme for Deutsche Bahn (German railways), including a family of corporate typefaces.

Spiekermann spoke about politics, and not simply in relation to the practice of design. The type of client is one thing, respect for the end-user another. However, having run small and large enterprises, he is also aware of the responsibilities that being an employer brings. Where do the quality of the working environment and the terms of employment fit in? Is it possible to be selective about how funds are generated and ensure that working processes are not abusive? These considerations are political too.

Erik Spiekermann

Erik Spiekermann was born in Stadthagen, Germany, in 1947. He studied history of art in Berlin, financing his studies by running a basement printing operation. On graduating, he moved to London where he worked as a consultant to various design companies and lectured at several colleges, including the London College of Printing. He returned to Berlin in 1981.

He describes himself as an information architect and type designer. In 1979 he founded MetaDesign. This is now Germany's largest design firm. Projects have included the design of the new passenger information system for the Berlin public transport corporations and the signage system at Dusseldorf International airport, and corporate design programmes for Audi, Skoda, Volkswagen, Heidelberg Printing and others. In July, 2000, Spiekermann withdrew from the management of MetaDesign Berlin. In 2001, he was commissioned to redesign *The Economist* magazine in London.

Spiekermann works both as a typographer and type designer. In 1988 he started FontShop, a company for the production and distribution of electronic fonts, and he has designed many typefaces himself, including FF Meta, ITC Officina, FF Info, FF Unit, LoType and Berliner Grotesk. Some of his latest fonts have received acclaim as modern classics. A corporate font family for Nokia was released in 2002.

Spiekermann holds an honorary professorship at the Academy of Arts in Bremen, is a board member of ATypI and the German Design Council, and is president of the ISTD (International Society of Typographic Designers). He is the author of many books and articles on type and typography. His most successful book, *Stop Stealing Sheep*, was published by Adobe Press in 1993 and has recently appeared in a second edition. He contributes to seminars, lectures and educational events that take him all over the world. Spiekermann is a signatory of the First Things First manifesto 2000.

Spiekermann's new studio, United Designers Network, was launched in 2002, and is currently designing the corporate design programmes for Bosch and Deutsche Bahn (German railways), including families of corporate typefaces.

He lives and works in Berlin, London and San Francisco.

Meta is th Helvetica of the 90s

FF Info *Info* Display
FF Info *Info* Display
FF Info *Info* Display
FF Info *Info* Display
FF Info *Info* Display

NokiaSansLight
Regular**SemiBold**
NokiaCondensed
NokiaWide*Italic***Bold**
NokiaTitleSemi**TitleBold**
NokiaSerif Regular**Bold**

Erik Spiekermann is famous for his prolific font design, including FF Meta, 1985, one of the most popular typefaces of the computer era; FF Info, 1997, a highly legible typeface used for the Dusseldorf International airport project; and Nokia Sans, 2002, a corporate typeface for Nokia based on bitmaps of phone screen fonts.

left to right
FF Info, 1997, was designed specifically for orientation systems and includes a complete set of pictograms, based on the typeface. Many of Spiekermann's fonts have been designed with applications in mind and some, like FF Meta, have become modern classics.

LoType **1979**
Berliner **Grotesk** 1980
FF Meta **1985**
FF Meta*Condensed* **1998**
ITC Officina**Sans** 1989
ITC Officina**Serif** 1989
FF Info*Display* **1997**
FF Info *Text* **1997**
FF Info**Office** **1998**
Glasgow 1999
Heidelberg **Gothic** 1999
ITC Officina**Display** 2001
Nokia**Sans** NokiaSerif 2002
FF Unit **2003**
FF MetaLight 2003
Bosch**Sans ...**

Spiekermann has found that large commercial clients respect the expertise of the designer. MetaDesign began working with Audi in 1994, developing a creative and strategic corporate identity programme for the company that included everything from complex design manuals to the simplification of the Audi logo.

Erik Spiekermann strives for clarity in thought and in deed. His ideals are tempered by a mistrust of simplistic political ideologies and theories that can destroy pragmatism and tolerance. 'First Things First is my theory,' he explains. 'My practice is that faced with the decision to sack ten people or take on a job for an evil empire, I'm not going to sack ten people.'

For Spiekermann, the relationship between politics and design is multifaceted. In his experience, clients who represent political organisations or social causes are often unprofessional and ill-informed about the value of good design. As if to add insult to injury not only are the fees poor, but so are the end results, because clients meddle detrimentally in the process and don't let designers do what they do best. 'I would love to only do work that is for the social good. I'd love to just improve social security applications and signage for the underground, I'd love it. There's so much rubbish out there because the public clients are the worst clients. I'd love to spend time educating them to communicate properly.'

Spiekermann is clear that some of the problem is 'design by committee'. It invariably reduces design potential however democratic it may at first appear to be. 'Commercial clients are better clients than the social clients. They tend to employ experts who know what they want. Whereas if you work for the council or similar, five people come to a meeting because they all need to be represented – the left, the middle and the right – and they just keep kicking each others' shins and disagreeing.'

Ironically, organisations in the public sector respect a designer more if they have commercial experience. 'If I had my choice I would always design bus schedules for public clients but I know they will take me more seriously because I've been successful at business. I can say – I did it for Audi, I can do it for you.'

The other option is to be hard-headed about the relationship between money and power. In Spiekermann's experience, it is often better to do social or arts projects for free, and retain power, than to end up compromised on all fronts. 'We do work for a theatre in Berlin that has no money. It is better that they don't pay at all so that they're not a client. We're saying we know how to do this. You don't, that's why you have come to us. We just do one presentation and that's it.'

Spiekermann considers that he has an obligation to those that he employs. 'We created an environment where people work fairly. Not without repression, there's always repression; I mean you work for a client and there are deadlines and there are constraints in the budget. But there was always the best equipment, the best espresso machine, the best space, the best colleagues, the best environment for the graphic designer.'

In contrast, working for the public sector can result in 'design by committee'. United Designers Network chose to work for free with the Shakespeare Company Berlin, 2004, thereby retaining creative freedom and control. Everything was designed as templates so the company can produce their own leaflets and posters.

Clients perceive this approach to be successful and are impressed, employees feel valued, are grateful, work harder and generate more profit. What business can be sustained without profit? Spiekermann identifies a more worrying problem, a shift in focus away from the work to the pleasure of the experience. 'What we did became almost secondary,' he explained. 'This was scary. We wouldn't have done propaganda for a war, but we did a cigarette pack at one time. In the end that's why I signed the manifesto. A job can seem so attractive that you forget that you are selling an evil product.'

For Spiekermann, self-expression is a political concern also. There is a deal struck between client and designer. Money is exchanged because the designer has a skill that the client requires. The important thing is to be clear about what that skill actually is and what the client thinks they have bought, otherwise it risks being an act of misrepresentation. 'The existential reason why we're not artists is that we only work for clients, we don't work for ourselves by and large. An artist expresses his or her view of the world. We don't. By definition I express my client's view. It doesn't mean I don't have one and it doesn't mean I don't bring it to bear. But I know that I'm in it because I get paid by somebody. There's no kidding myself. I'm not in it to express myself. Self-expression for me is a red herring.'

This touches on issues of professionalism. If a designer undertakes a commission, regardless of what it is, are they not morally obligated to do it well? 'Even if you work for car manufacturers or telephone companies that responsibility is still there,' suggests Spiekermann. 'Even if you're only fulfilling their marketing hype. It can be done badly, it can be done well, if only from a craft point of view. As the saying goes – if something is worth doing, it is worth doing well.'

Some of Spiekermann's views are unfashionable, but he is no stranger to criticism. He does not set out to be subversive and yet seems to take some pleasure in being slightly detached from the world of graphic design. A detachment that he puts down to the circuitous route he took to get there. 'The previous generation hated me because I was loudmouthed, opinionated, and I had come from nowhere. I hadn't been to Ulm, I had no degree in graphic design. I'm an art historian. Architectural historian actually.'

The diversity of his practice merely compounded these attitudes. 'I started approaching work from a more modernist perspective; rational, information design work, and those Ulm people started loving me but the book designers hated me. They had liked me before because I had previously worked sensitively with older typefaces. The corporate design guys don't like me very much because I do other things as well, whilst the real type designers don't like me because I work on type designs as a more collective effort which threatens their position. Now the modernist German information designers think my work is too flamboyant. Whereas the flamboyant people think it really boring. I don't have a theory to apply. I do have a rational approach, but that's because I like science and because I have an academic background I suppose.'

When it comes to developing theories that feed usefully into design practice Spiekermann is sceptical. 'The fact that theories change proves that none of them are true, but theory serves two functions. One is it can give you a position from which to start the process. The other way to use theory is, of course, for post-rationalisation. I guess after years of application the post-rationalisation can be said to become the theory.'

Bus stops before and after the implementation of MetaDesign's information system for the Berlin Transit Authority, 1990–94. The reunification of Germany prompted the need for a new passenger information and transit system for the whole city, including signage for 6,700 bus and tram stops, 251 bus and tram routes and 170 subway stations.

Spiekermann is well travelled. This experience, combined with his training as an historian, is useful to him in evaluating design theory and its worth. 'Britain has never been very theoretical about design. We Germans have been very theoretical, the Dutch have also and there's a small pocket in America. Britain is the nation of shopkeepers. You had one running the country for a long time – Maggie was a greengrocer's daughter. Things are bought and sold. You put a price on them and that's it. The Brits have always been very pragmatic about it in a good and a bad sense.'

Spiekermann values pragmatism even in his assessment of himself. He knows his strengths and weaknesses and is confident enough to express them. 'I instantly recognise a pattern, whether it's a language, whether it's in people, whether it's in communication or a conversation, in the boardroom. That's my talent. I know exactly what's needed. I do sketches, I do the structure and I do the grid. I love the mathematical approach. I get great joy out of coming back to the studio, briefing all these great people and then their results always stun me. I would have done something very pedestrian, very predictable, very functional, very German, but it wouldn't have any elegance, it wouldn't have any lightness.'

For Spiekermann, graphic design is political because it operates in the public domain. 'It's political because it is what people see. They don't see the truth or the content. They see design. We build a form of reality for people.' Regardless of the type of product the approach to aesthetics is political too. 'We have a responsibility. It's like air, you know, the only time we ever talk about it is when it's threatened and the only time normal people ever talk about graphic design is when it doesn't work. It can always be more aesthetic, whatever that means, even fashion has a contribution there. And function, even fun is a function. Why should things be ugly, and why should things be illegible? Maybe that's as political as it gets.'

Erik Spiekermann does not set out to challenge the status quo, but he is no less aware of the political issues that surround his practice than any other more visibly subversive political designer. He believes in education to ensure that young designers know about 'culture, background, where things come from, why things look the way they look and how what we do affects the world and other people.'

'For me the manifesto is a wish list,' he concludes. 'We take on a lot of jobs that aren't furthering the common good, but we live in a capitalist society and I'm not going to change that society by denying my designers access to it.'

As a U-Bahn user Spiekermann felt insulted by the lack of consideration given to passengers' concerns and by the apparent absence of any professional design activity on the transit system. MetaDesign created a coherent identity across stations, signage and livery that functioned effectively and in sympathy with the local environment.

MetaDesign's work for
the Berlin Transit Authority
included providing detailed style
manuals for in-house designers
allowing personnel to update
information such as maps
and timetables and liberating
them from dependency on
external agencies. Creating
a rationalised system meant
that for the first time since
1961 all subway and regional
train connections could
be shown in one diagram.

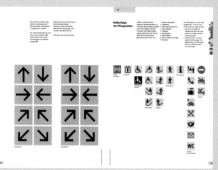

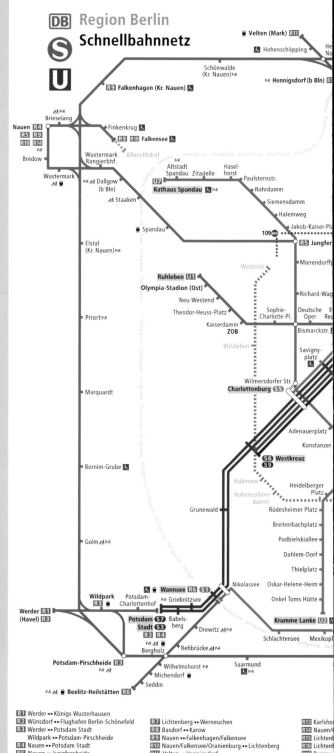

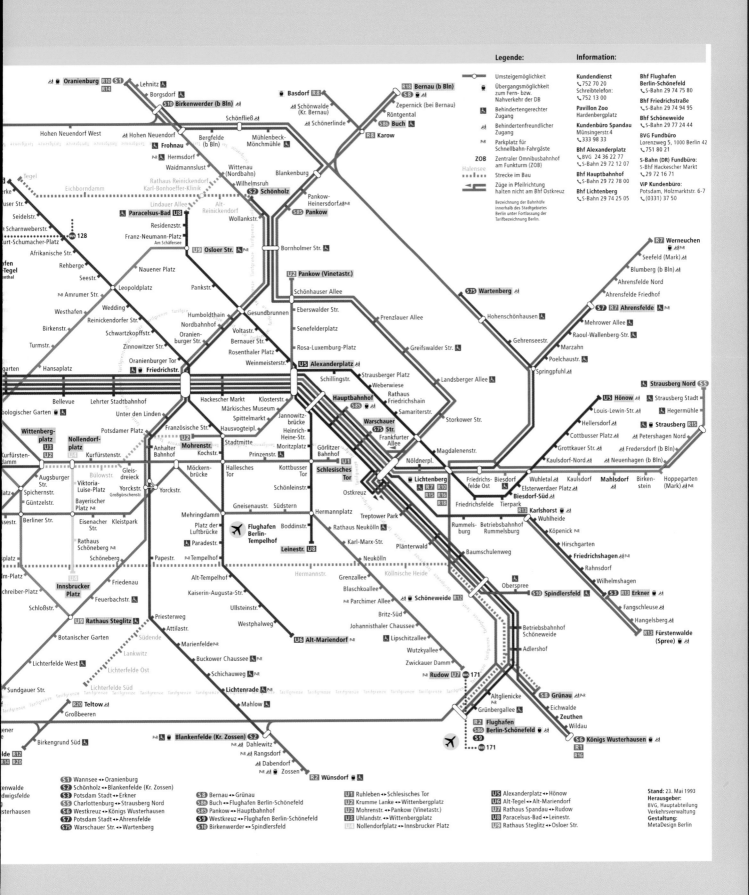

In 2001, Spiekermann redesigned *The Economist* magazine. Previously dense and difficult to navigate, Spiekermann improved the accessibility and legibility of the magazine through scrutiny of typographic detail and hierarchical structures. This led to the introduction of clarifying subtitles, contrasting weights and colour to enhance navigation.

With Ole Schaefer, Spiekermann altered both the text font and titling face by removing unnecessary detail that caused visual noise in small sizes. ITC Officina Sans was chosen as the 'information' typeface for captions, tables and navigation, but at large sizes was deemed too 'goofy' by the client. A new version, ITC Officina Display, was designed and used for the front cover.

Inside, the contents page was expanded to include article titles, subtitles and graphics and the new layout separated editorial content and navigation. The contrast of old and new is evident here: the redesigned cover and contents page appear on the left.

IT IS daunting to
how much turns
tion of American
Stockmarket valua
even now by his
dards: global finan

market valuat
now by histe
global financ
tlook for livin

The new fonts were specifically designed for *The Economist*'s printing process. They are shown here as enlargements from a printed page. The panel, right, shows the old and new text faces.

Hafnegi1no3
Hafnegi1ɴo3
Hafnegi1o3
Hafnegi1o3

These two editorial spreads from *The Economist* clearly demonstrate the improvement after Spiekermann's redesign. The recent spread, below, uses more white space and bolder navigation, bringing immediate visual clarity to the page. Section openers now have their own mini content-listing for easier navigation.

Informations- und Leitsystem Flughaf

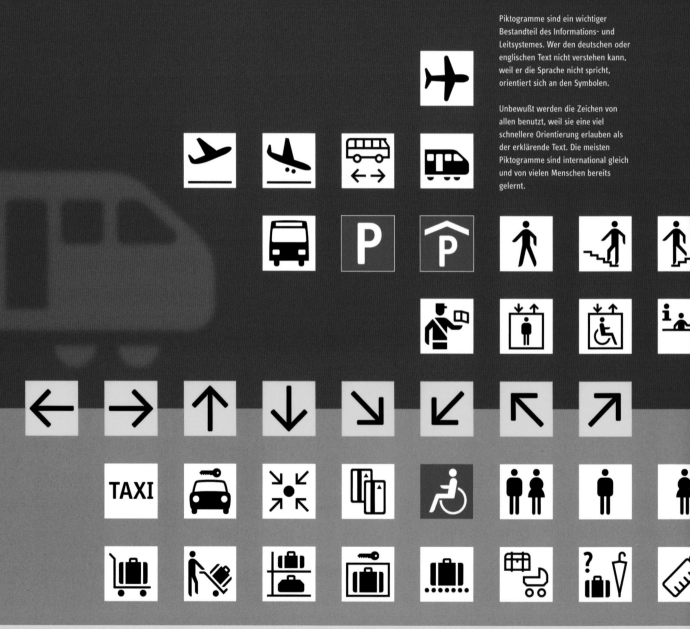

Piktogramme sind ein wichtiger
Bestandteil des Informations- und
Leitsystemes. Wer den deutschen oder
englischen Text nicht verstehen kann,
weil er die Sprache nicht spricht,
orientiert sich an den Symbolen.

Unbewußt werden die Zeichen von
allen benutzt, weil sie eine viel
schnellere Orientierung erlauben als
der erklärende Text. Die meisten
Piktogramme sind international gleich
und von vielen Menschen bereits
gelernt.

Düsseldorf

MetaDesign developed a complete corporate design system for Dusseldorf International airport following a catastrophic fire in 1996. Spiekermann utilised his new font FF Info, designed specifically for orientation systems and highly legible due to its narrow letterforms and open spacing. The blunt corners on the letters and pictograms allow for clarity even when backlit and the conically shaped signage hardware reduces blurring of information and increases legibility when viewed in motion.

Emmi Salonen

Biography

Emmi Salonen was born in Turku, Finland, in 1977. In 1997, she moved to London to undertake a foundation course in art and design. As a graphic design student at the University of Brighton in the UK, Salonen was frustrated by a lack of political engagement. Before graduating she applied to Fabrica, the Benetton Research and Development Communication Centre in Italy, hoping to find a forum in which to combine politics with further creative studies and practice. She was accepted by Fabrica and took up a year's grant-aided place in 2001.

Fabrica's best known output is *Colors* magazine. Founded ten years ago, under the direction of Tibor Kalman, it is based on the conviction that all cultures have the same value and that difference is a richness to be protected. Fabrica selects young artists, designers and researchers from all over the world and invites them to participate in a range of communication activities in cinema, photography, graphics, design or music, as part of *Colors* magazine, or within the interactive department. Learning is through hands-on involvement in real multidisciplinary projects.

In 2002, Salonen returned to the UK, working for two years at Hoop Associates, a design practice specialising in work for the voluntary sector. Clients included ippr (Institute for Public Policy Research), Transport for London and the Crown Prosecution Service. In 2004, Salonen moved to New York and worked as a graphic designer at Karlssonwilker on a variety of projects, including a book on architecture for Phaidon Press and a corporate identity for a gallery.

Salonen's work has been published in a variety of books and magazines including *Mail Me*, a book about mail art published by Electa, and *Size Matters: Effective Graphic Design for Large Amounts of Information* published by RotoVision. Her work has also been shown in *Visions of Change*, a book by Fabrica and has been commissioned by *CosmoGirl*, *Mute* and *Internazionale* magazines.

She has contributed to group exhibitions in Tokyo, Osaka, Lisbon, London and in various cities throughout Italy, Holland and France.

This selection of Salonen's work shows her ongoing commitment to producing socially engaged work. Latterly, Salonen has worked at Karlssonwilker in New York. Here, she feels relatively uncompromised politically by working on art-based projects. Shown here are test designs for an architecture book, 2005.

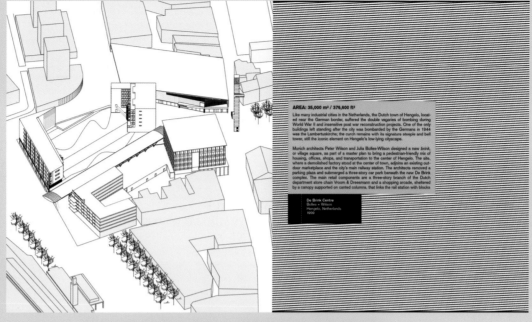

AREA: 35,000 m² / 376,600 ft²

Like many industrial cities in the Netherlands, the Dutch town of Hengelo, located near the German border, suffered the double vagaries of bombing during World War II and insensitive post war reconstruction projects. One of the only buildings left standing after the city was bombarded by the Germans in 1944 was the Lambertuskirche; the church remains with its signature steeple and bell tower, still the iconic element on Hengelo's low-lying cityscape.

Munich architects Peter Wilson and Julia Bolles-Wilson designed a new brink, or village square, as part of a master plan to bring a pedestrian-friendly mix of housing, offices, shops, and transportation to the center of Hengelo. The site, where a demolished factory stood at the center of town, adjoins an existing outdoor marketplace and the city's main railway station. The architects removed a parking plaza and submerged a three-story car park beneath the new De Brink complex. The main retail components are a three-story branch of the Dutch department store chain Vroom & Dreesmann and a shopping arcade, sheltered by a canopy supported on canted columns, that links the rail station with blocks

De Brink Centre
Bolles + Wilson
Hengelo, Netherlands
1999

"It has been an incredible year, and more changes are on the way."

Financial review

Salonen studied graphic design in the UK. She was shocked by the high rates of teenage pregnancy and in 2001 produced the animation, *A Woman's Place*, in which she asked whether for many poorly educated young women this is the only way to have a sense of identity.

commoncause

yess
Youth Education Support Services

Luke Lawrence
91 High Street
Camberwell
SE5 7LB London
T 020 7920 5823
F 020 7920 5824

Salonen worked for two years at Hoop Associates, London, who specialise in design for the voluntary sector. Examples of her work there include the 2003 annual report for the charity Crisis, which helps homeless people, and the logo for Common Cause, a consultancy giving business and marketing advice to organisations, including charities. Salonen volunteered to produce design for Youth Education Support Services (Yess), 2003. The charity aims to give young people in south London a voice through education.

In 2001, Salonen worked at Fabrica in Treviso, Italy. Whilst there, Salonen produced a video self-portrait; her reaction to the numerous examples of right-wing graffiti in the nearby environment. Salonen made a large stencil of a girl and a bin, which she spray-painted in fluorescent pink on top of the swastikas.

Emmi Salonen has been trying to find a way to express her political engagement through some kind of professional practice from an early age. 'Growing up I was involved in demonstrations. I started thinking what to do and considered social work, but it was way too heavy for me. In graphic design it is possible to help people, but keep an emotional distance.'

This has not been a straightforward option. With each new graphic design experience Salonen redefines her methods though her objectives remain the same. She moves within the territory between self-initiated work and commercial practice, hoping to find some middle ground in which to be active, useful and also pay the bills.

'I'm still learning and seeing what works. It's very important for me to be happy as well, for myself, for the people around me. That goes for every designer – you have to find your own way, asking what it is that you want from being a socially aware designer. Then you consider how to fulfil these objectives and weigh up how much engagement is enough for you.'

In 1997, Salonen came to Britain from her native Finland, first taking a foundation course and then studying graphic design at the University of Brighton. While on the course she felt rather alone with her political ideas. 'I did a lot of personal work outside the course as the briefs weren't directed towards my interests. I would try to bring an environmental or social issue into my work. First Things First was mentioned, but nobody was interested in talking about it with me. It was really upsetting, isolating in many senses. But Lawrence Zeegan, who ran the course, was really encouraging and he kept telling me to do what I wanted to do.'

Coming from Finland, Salonen was depressed by some of what she saw in British culture, a focus on individualism that she feels prevails particularly within media and design. 'In England, youth culture is focused on fame and personal success. Designers are almost like rock stars. The result is quite a few designers who end up miserable and disappointed because they haven't "made it". But is this really the goal that you should set yourself when you start working as a designer?'

The emphasis on individual success and acquisition is hardly surprising in the UK. For years, help for the disadvantaged had been gradually diminished. People are encouraged to take responsibility for themselves, but this engenders fear and an isolationist mentality. In Salonen's experience, the Nordic model is preferable. 'In the Nordic countries living standards are higher, education is really good and young people study sociology and environmental issues and they're worried about them and talk about them. It's much more outward-looking. Maybe this is partly because the social security system is still adequate and intact. People feel more supported and secure. When I compare people who don't have money in England with similar people in Finland, they're different.'

In Britain, Salonen felt that socially orientated design was marginalised: 'It's only ever featured as a special issue,' she comments. So, towards the latter part of her time at Brighton, Salonen started to investigate moving within Europe again, this time to Italy, and applied to Fabrica. Fabrica takes young artists and designers on relatively short contracts. The emphasis is on learning through hands-on involvement in real multidisciplinary and commercial projects.

Salonen was lucky. Usually applicants send their portfolios and may have to wait some time before being invited to come for a two-week trial period. Even if they are successful their contract may only be for three months, some of which takes the form of further trials. 'I sent my portfolio and I was really lucky because I think Omar Vulpinari was looking for someone like me for the department,' explains Salonen. 'He wanted me to go there straight away on a contract. I left university and a month later I was working at Fabrica.'

'It was great to go there,' says Salonen, 'it allowed me to do completely political and social work.' Whilst there, she was involved in the design of various items to be sold in the Fabrica shops, produced several illustrations for different magazines and worked on awareness raising campaigns about issues, such as drunken driving.

But Salonen doubted some of the relevance of her approach to work at Fabrica. Gradually, she became aware of how removed she was from real-world design practice. 'It was self-indulgent. I could just express my own opinions. It's great to be able to do that, but it's not actually really helping anyone. Lots of people leave Fabrica and have nothing to go to. They struggle for quite a while with the change because it's not like the real world when you work there because you're so free.' She was offered another year-long contract at Fabrica, but at the same time a London design group also offered her a job. Hoop Associates specialise in work for the public sector and so this seemed like the right move. 'I saw it as an opportunity to really give it a go and work hard,' explains Salonen. 'I don't think design is art and I don't mind that at all,' she adds.

This experience threw up new concerns for Salonen. Obviously, as is often the case with this kind of work, she was constrained by tight budgets and cautious clients who had a very limited vision, but these were not the real worries for Salonen. 'To start with I was really interested and happy to deal with the people who worked in this field because they had a passion for it,' she explains. 'However, after about two years I realised that the work was a difficult hybrid of something altruistically motivated and yet still commercial.'

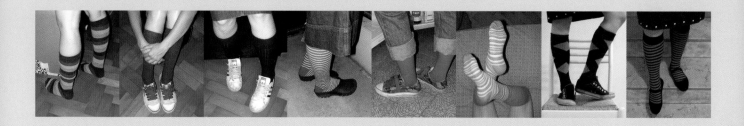

Salonen felt forced to reassess her attitude to work again. If the voluntary and public sectors are simply a market like any other then perhaps it is better to accept the relationship between design and money. She can still feel relatively uncompromised politically by working commercially for art-based clients and then donate time to worthy causes. 'I'd much rather work for galleries and publishers and then donate my own time for free to work for socially orientated organisations. That's the direction I'm going in at the moment. I need to work for money like everyone has to. I'm still trying to do that in a field where I don't feel like a complete sell-out, where I feel that I've got my morals. But I can also use the skills that I have and donate my time. Fabrica changed me and working in London changed me. I realised that I didn't have to do work about anti-globalisation or war to be social and political.'

Salonen went on to work at a small agency in New York called Karlssonwilker. Most of its clients are in the music industry, but other clients include a property developer, restaurants, galleries and publishers. 'They produce very quirky and funny stuff,' explains Salonen. 'I'm having a lot of fun designing and I have to say I think it's a lot to do with the people, not only about the work. At the moment I'm full-time here and then I do my freelance work through contacts I have in Europe. So now I'm really working for money, but I'm still not selling my soul.'

The attitude in New York feeds Salonen's approach to work. 'I get involved in the local scene, what's going on within the liberal movements in New York, how they deal with their problems in their communities. There are so many designers and artists here, but the approach is open, they always let new people in. It's much more inspiring, I think. It's not such a closed design community as it is in London.'

Salonen's journey has brought her back to considering some core concerns. She wanted to make a difference in the lives of lots of different types of people. 'I produce work on my own and sell it in shops. I get a reaction from normal people, that was the whole point of my starting to do graphic design. To say something, have influence and get a reaction.' She is clear that for her the appeal of graphic design lies in the potential breadth of its audience. 'Who are we designing for?' she asks. 'Are we designing for other designers, their appreciation, or are we designing for the people?'

I HAVE IT ALL

top
A self-initiated project, 2002, in which Salonen uses her socks as a metaphor for consumption and desire. As with many objects, once bought, each pair is subsumed in the collection and forgotten along with the rest.

THIS YEAR I WILL:

_____

_____

_____

above
Two cards designed by Salonen at Fabrica, 2002. The top is a comment on the consumerism of Christmas whilst the other invites users to consider their promises for the coming year.

right
Since being a student Salonen has produced and designed badges; the traditional icon of political agitation. These have ranged from her News Icon series, 2001, designed to bring awareness of current affairs to young people, to her Poplitics range of 2004, which carry provocative slogans such as 'make oil not love'.

events and repercussions of 11 September, 2001. Salonen's illustrations explore the media's response, the west's new insecurity and the growing fear and religious hatred. The cover, left, was designed by Georges Chartier.

44. 45.

Whilst at Fabrica, Salonen designed this highly inventive anti-drinking and driving campaign, 2002. Her proposal included placing life-size cut-outs of accident victims on the front windows of cars parked near to nightclubs, and sealing car doors with thought-provoking stickers.

A series of booklets designed by Salonen during her period at Hoop Associates for the Crown Prosecution Service, 2003–04. Produced for internal use only, Salonen used a colour-coding system for easy navigation allied to clear and simple typography and produced an accessible, but suitably formal set of publications.

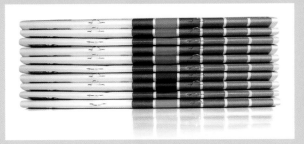

Salonen designed the identity for the Goldman Warehouse gallery in New York whilst at Karlssonwilker, 2004–05. The gallery exhibits private collections of abstract art and Salonen's identity is an appropriately sophisticated solution that makes a subtle reference to the marks left on the walls whilst absent paintings are away from home.

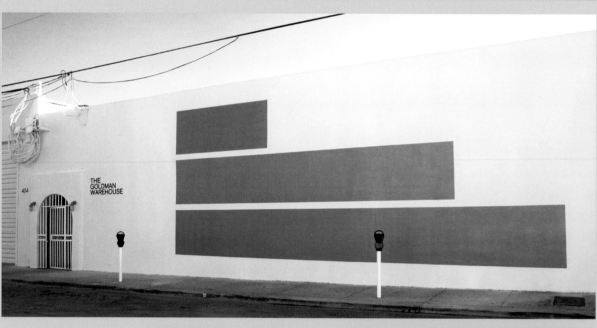

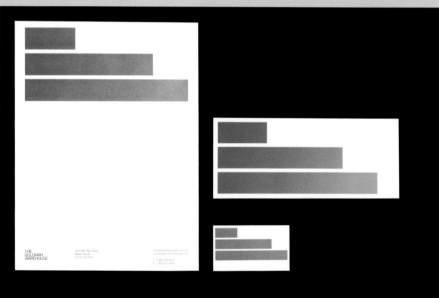

In 2005, Salonen designed the end of year catalogue for the Contemporary Media Course at London's University of Westminster. Salonen used single and full colour on a mix of paper stocks to reflect the diverse nature of the student work, whilst producing a publication that is visually cohesive to emphasise the equality of the group.

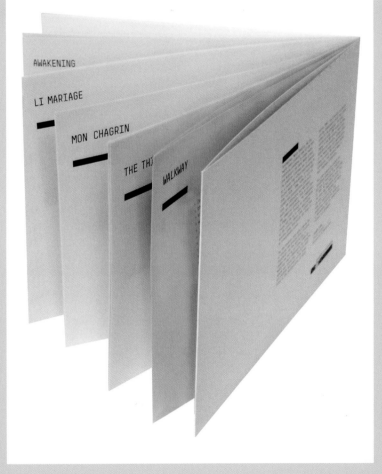

03   Questions in summary

01 What issues concern you about your role or future role as a designer?

02 Is it possible to be an ethical designer and still develop a career?

03 Some law firms allow staff to take on 'pro bono' cases (for free, for the public good) to balance their paid work. Would such a scheme work in design? Or should the public's good be at the core of all activity?

04 What do your parents and friends think design is? Can you explain why it is worth studying? Can anyone be a designer?

05 What is your reaction to the idea that design is at risk of alienating itself through allying itself with attitudes of the art world?

06 Salonen says that politics weren't formally discussed enough on her course. In the introduction to this book I suggest that politics should be integrated into every aspect. What is your experience and opinion on this? Should design education be about how design operates within society, or should it be about how to do design? Or both?

07 Spiekermann points out that theories change and that they are often used to post-rationalise design. But he calls for breadth of teaching, which would include the sort of theory discussed in this book. Neville Brody says essentially the same thing. How do you feel about this issue?

ISBN-13: 978-2-940373-09-3
ISBN-10: 2-940373-09-4
90000>
EAN
9 782940 373093

PANTONE®
4/C Process   Solid Color

| PANTONE® OOZO-C | PANTONE Proc. Yellow C |
| C:0.0 M:0.0 Y:100.0 K:0.0 | |

| PANTONE® OZOO-C | PANTONE Proc. Magen. C |
| C:0.0 M:100.0 Y:0.0 K:0.0 | |

| PANTONE® ZOOO-C | PANTONE Proc. Cyan C |
| C:100.0 M:0.0 Y:0.0 K:0.0 | |

| PANTONE® OOOZ-C | PANTONE Proc. Black C |
| C:0.0 M:0.0 Y:0.0 K:100.0 | |

| PANTONE® OMWO-C | PANTONE Orange 021 C |

| PANTONE® OXWO-C | PANTONE Red 032 C |
| C:0.0 M:91.0 Y:87.0 K:0.0 | |

| PANTONE® ZUOO-C | PANTONE Blue 072 C |
| C:100.0 M:79.0 Y:0.0 K:0.0 | |

Design/photography biographies

Design/art direction

Bob Wilkinson graduated from Central St Martins College of Art and Design in 1993 and started work at Neville Brody's Research Studios. Whilst there he worked on a range of projects, including an annual report for Zumtobel Lighting, and packaging for the software company Macromedia. After four years he joined Lucienne Roberts at sans+baum where he is involved in a broad range of projects, from arts- to charity-related work. He has taught at the London College of Communication, Camberwell School of Art and is a senior lecturer at Buckinghamshire Chilterns University College. Wilkinson is a signatory of the First Things First 2000 manifesto, a call for greater awareness of design responsibility.

Photography

Andrew Penketh studied fine art at Camberwell and Chelsea School of Art. His drawings won first prize at the Nuremberg Triennial in addition to having an extensive exhibition in London. From 1989 to 1993, he worked as assistant to Anish Kapoor. During this period he turned to photography to document his travels and was encouraged by his early work with Graphic Thought Facility to follow photography as a career. His clients have included Habitat, Harvey Nichols and American Express. He is currently working on a Central St Martins' funded, practice-based research project on architectural drawing and Julia Kristeva's notion of poetry and the perception of space.

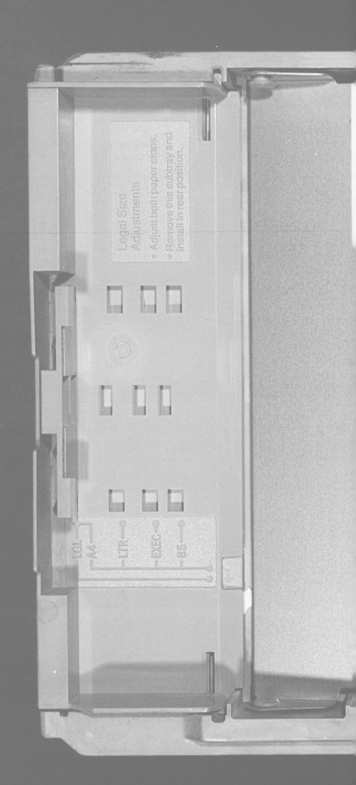

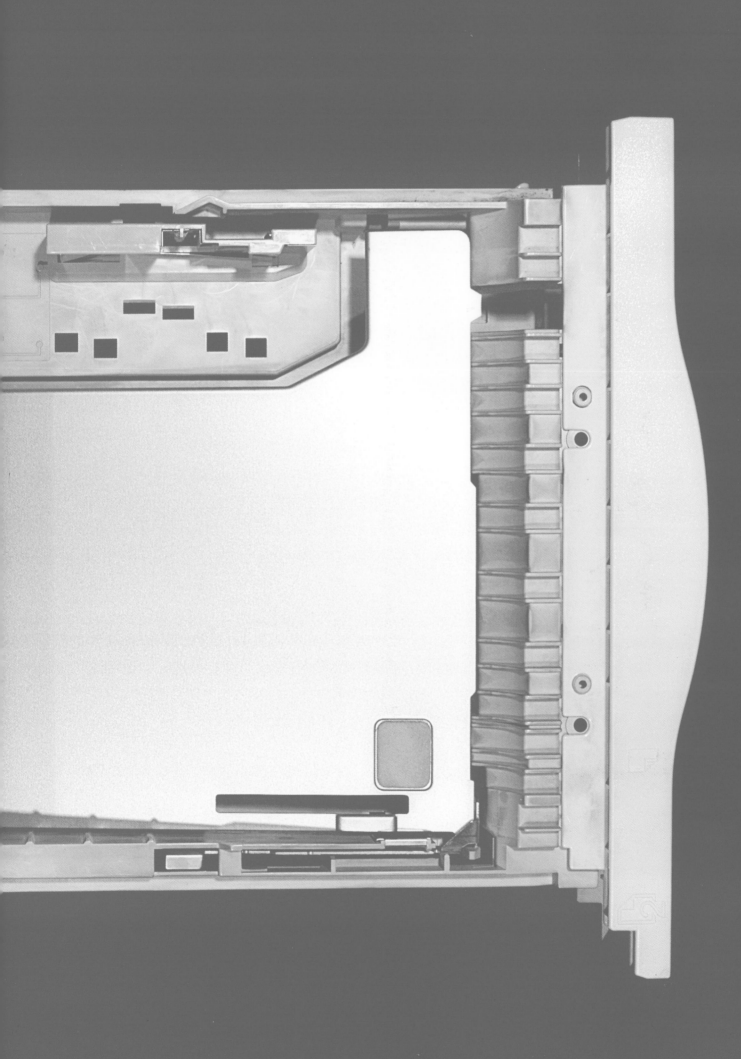

Bibliography

Baudrillard, Jean
**For a Critique of the Political
Economy of the Sign**
Telos Press Ltd
1983

Bennett, Tony, Grossberg,
Lawrence, et al., Eds
**New Keywords:
A Revised Vocabulary of
Culture and Society**
Oxford, Blackwell Publishing
2005

Berger, Arthur Asa
**Ads, Fads and Consumer
Culture: Advertising's
Impact on American
Character and Society**
Oxford, Rowman and Littlefield
2000

Carey, John
What Good Are the Arts?
London, Faber and Faber
2005

Chandler, Daniel
Semiotics: The Basics
London, Routledge
2002

Crow, David
Visible Sign
Lausanne, AVA Publishing
2004

Dawkins, Richard
The Selfish Gene
Oxford, Oxford University Press
1989

Dyer, Gillian
Advertising as Communication
London, Routledge
1982

Fiske, John
**Introduction to
Communication Studies**
London, Routledge
1990

Heller, Stephen
The Graphic Design Reader
New York, Allworth Press
2002

Justice, Lorraine
**The Big Squeeze:
The Education of
a Graphic Designer**
S. Heller, Ed.
New York, Allworth Press
1998

Klein, Naomi
No Logo
London, Flamingo
2000

Lane, Richard J
**Routledge Critical Thinkers:
Jean Baudrillard**
London, Routledge
2000

Lasn, Kalle
**Culture Jam:
The Uncooling of America**
New York, Eagle Brook
2000

Lechte, John
**Fifty Key Contemporary
Thinkers: From Structuralism
to Postmodernity**
London, Routledge
1994

Noble, Ian and Bestley, Russell
Visual Research
Lausanne, AVA Publishing
2005

O'Sullivan, Tim, Hartley,
John, et al, Eds
**Key Concepts in
Communication and
Cultural Studies**
London, Routledge
1994

Papanek, Victor
**Design for the Real
World: Human Ecology
and Social Change**
London, Thames and Hudson
1985

Storey, John
**An Introduction to Cultural
Theory and Popular Culture**
London, Prentice Hall
1993

Watson, James and Hill,
Anne, Eds
**Dictionary of Communication
and Media Studies**
London, Hodder Arnold
2003

Weaver, W and Shannon, CE
**The Mathematical Theory
of Communication**
Urbana, Illinois,
University of Illinois Press
1949

Williamson, Judith
**Decoding Advertisements:
Ideology and Meaning
in Advertising**
London, Marion Boyars
1978

Wolf, Alison
**Does Education Matter?
Myths about Education
and Economic Growth**
London, Penguin
2002

Index

Index

Index

Credits

The Theory

Page 26–27
Thank you to David Harrison
for modelling the gesture images

Page 30
Close up of a middle aged man
AT4B7A
Ingram Publishing/Alamy

People
AP3D65
Design Pics Inc./Alamy

AC292F
Inmagine/Alamy

Page 40
Two high school girls
in uniform stand on the
street and chat
A8612B
Photo Japan/Alamy

Page 41
19th Century: A Portrait of
the German founder of modern
communism Karl Marx
A51D05
POPPERFOTO/Alamy

Page 74
AY7785
Photofusion Picture Library/
Alamy

Page 75
Family gathering in living room
AY7519
Janine Wiedel Photolibrary/
Alamy

Page 79
Charmin Bear logo with
thanks and acknowledgement
to Procter & Gamble UK

Andrex with thanks and
acknowledgement to Andrex

Skoda Octavia Combi 'Verlieben'
With thanks and acknowledge-
ment to Leagas Delaney
Hamburg GmbH

© Skoda Auto Deutschland GmbH

Page 83
AB33AA
SHOUT/Alamy

A6M02E
geogphotos/Alamy

Page 94
AR22C7
AK PhotoLibrary/Alamy

Pages 96–97
A4D23F
POPPERFOTO/Alamy

A6REA6
Buzz Pictures/Alamy

A4D82E
POPPERFOTO/Alamy

AP0179
Lyndon Giffard/Alamy

Page 130
Wind-up radio designed
by Trevor Bayliss
© Freeplay Energy Plc

Page 136
Thank you to Ian Wright
for billboard image

Pages 132–133
Chair
With thanks and
acknowledgement to
Herman Miller Limited

Pages 137–140
www.adbusters.org

Page 141
S.O.S!
Anthony Garner

Protestors on roof
EMPICS/PA

Page 143
www.adbusters.org

Page 152
With thanks and
acknowledgement to
Sagmeister Inc.

All other photography
Andrew Penketh

The Practice

Interview transcription
Deirdre Murphy

**Additional writing
and research**
Rebecca Wright

Pages 60–61
Photography
Minnesota Children's
Museum signage
Don Wong

Page 113
Photography
Snowman Salt and Pepper
shakers
Robert Walker

Orbital WorkStation
c/o Keen

Cross Table
M Hirai

Muji crockery
H Yoshimura

Mandarine Oriental Spa
Shin Azumi

Page 115
Photography
Table = Chest
Thomas Dobbie

Pages 116–117
Photography
Muji crockery
H Yoshimura

Pages 118–119
Photography
Donkey 3
c/o Isokon Plus

ShipShape
Akio

Pages 120–121
Photography
ZA stools and Lem bar stool
c/o Lapalma

Page 122
Photography
Music Tube
M Hirai

Page 123
Photography
Wire Frame furniture
Julian Hawkins

Pages 160–171
Photography
Erik Spiekermann and
MetaDesign

Page 180
Photography
Exterior of Goldman Warehouse
Simon Hare Photography

All other photography
Andrew Penketh